The Junior Baker's Cook Sweet Treats and Creative Confections

~~belongs~~ to Dalia Alnaili

Step-by-Step Recipes for Cookies, Cakes, and More!

By Sharon D. Morgan

This book belongs to

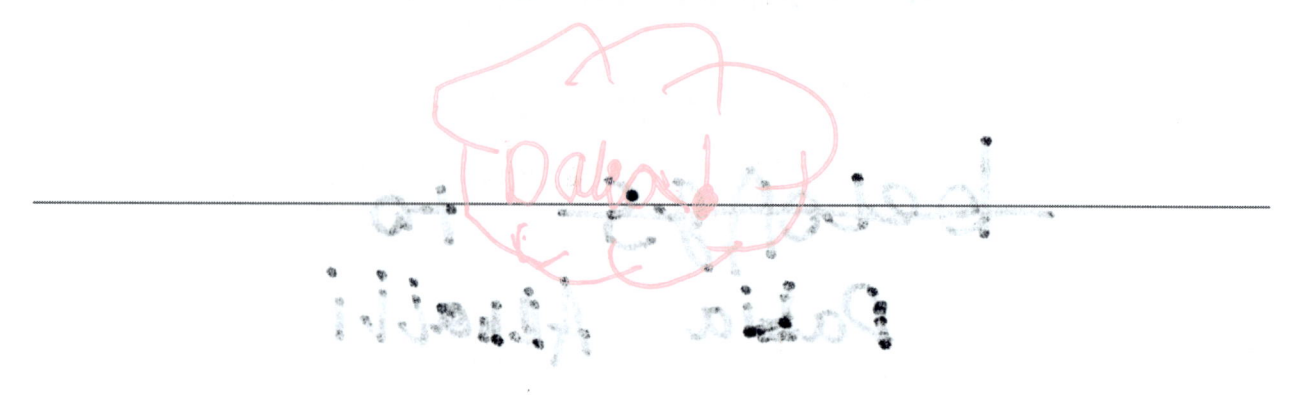

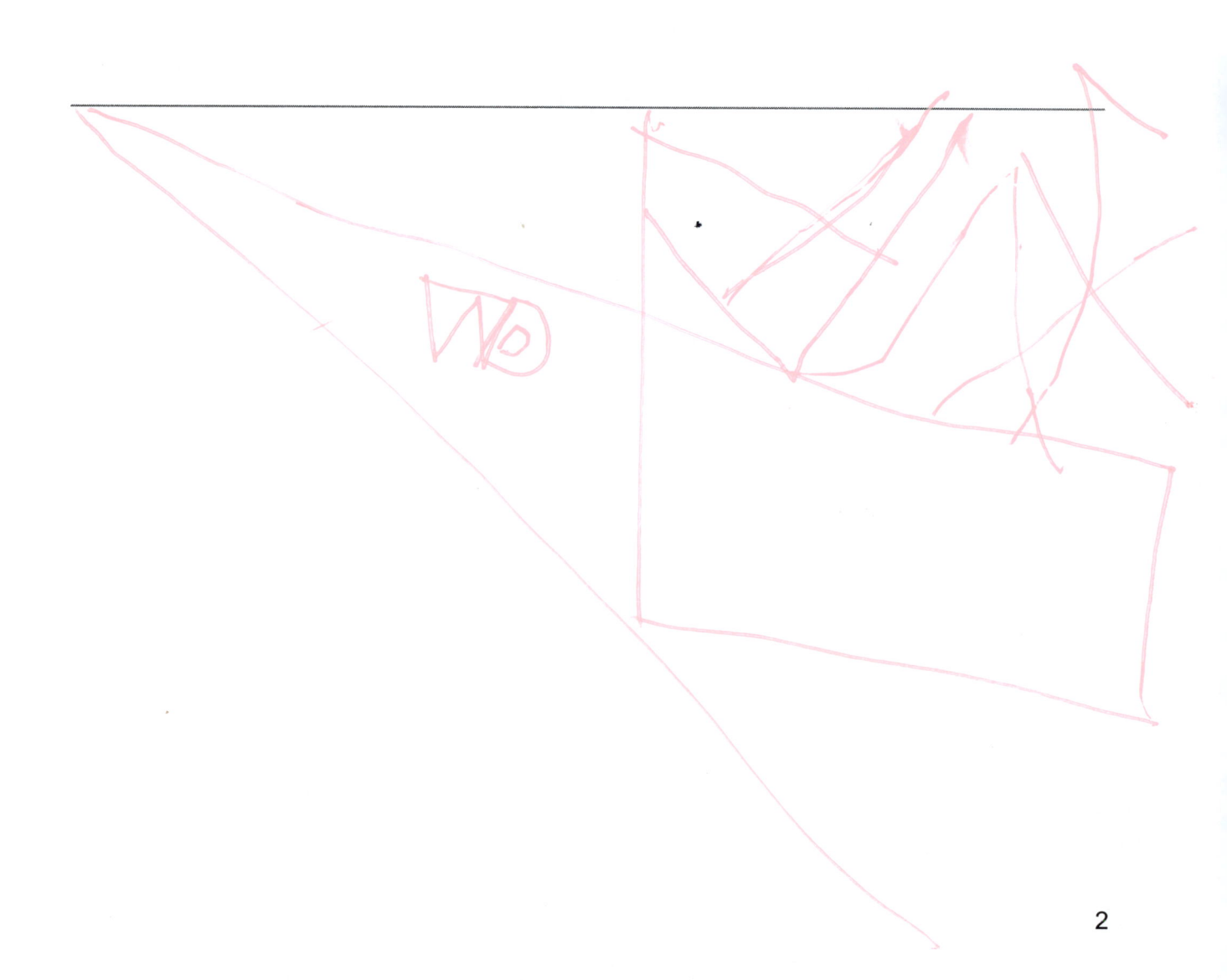

Copyright - 2023 by Sharon D. Morgan

All rights reserved.

No part of this book may be reproduced in any form without written permission from the publisher or author, except as permitted by U.S. copyright law.

TABLE OF CONTENTS

Preface..12
Introduction..16
   Welcome to the World of Junior Baking.. 16
A Brief Note to Parents and Guardians............................... 17
Kitchen Safety Tips for Young Bakers................................. 18
Essential Baking Tools and Ingredients............................. 21
Chapter 1: Cookie Creations... 28
   Classic Chocolate Chip Cookies.. 28
   Peanut Butter Blossom Cookies.. 32
   Sugar Sprinkle Cookies... 36
   Oatmeal Raisin Gems... 39
   Double Chocolate Chunk Brownie Cookies............................... 43
Chapter 2: Cupcake Delights... 48
   Vanilla Cupcakes with Buttercream Frosting............................. 48
   Chocolate Fudge Cupcakes.. 53
   Strawberry Swirl Cupcakes.. 58
   Funfetti Surprise Cupcakes.. 64
   Lemon Zest Cupcakes with Creamy Lemon Frosting................ 70
Chapter 3: Cake Magic... 77
   Rainbow Layer Cake with Whipped Cream Frosting..................77
   Marble Cake with Chocolate Ganache...................................... 83
   Red Velvet Cake with Cream Cheese Frosting......................... 89
   Raspberry Almond Cake... 94
   Carrot Cake with Creamy Maple Frosting................................. 100
Chapter 4: Sweet Breads and Muffins................................. 107
   Banana Nut Bread.. 107
   Blueberry Muffins.. 111
   Zucchini Chocolate Chip Bread... 114
   Cinnamon Swirl Muffins... 118
   Pumpkin Spice Muffins.. 124

Chapter 5: Fun and Fancy Treats..........130
- Homemade Pop Tarts..........130
- Mini Fruit Tarts..........135
- Chocolate-Dipped Pretzel Rods..........140
- Mini Cheesecakes with Fruit Topping..........143
- Cream Puffs with Vanilla Custard Filling..........148

Chapter 6: Creative Confections..........155
- Cake Pops: Bites of Joy..........155
  - A. Classic Chocolate Delight..........155
  - B. Strawberry Shortcake Bliss..........158
  - C. Cookies and Cream Euphoria..........162
  - D. Tropical Pineapple Paradise..........165
  - E. Cake Pop Creations to Try on Your Own..........168
- Rice Krispie Treats with a Twist..........172
- Decorated Sugar Cookies..........176
- Chocolate-Covered Marshmallow Pops..........181
- Fruit Kabobs with Yogurt Dip..........186

Chapter 7: Special Occasion Sensations..........190
- Mini Chocolate Fondue Party..........190
- Halloween Monster Cupcakes..........195
- Snowman Cake for Winter Celebrations..........199
- Easter Bunny Cake..........203
- Fourth of July Firework Cookies..........207
- Cake Parfait Delights..........211

Conclusion..........215
- Your Baking Adventure Continues!..........215
- Experimenting With Your Own Flavors and Ideas..........218
- Sharing Your Delicious Creations with Friends and Family..........222

Let's Bake it kids!

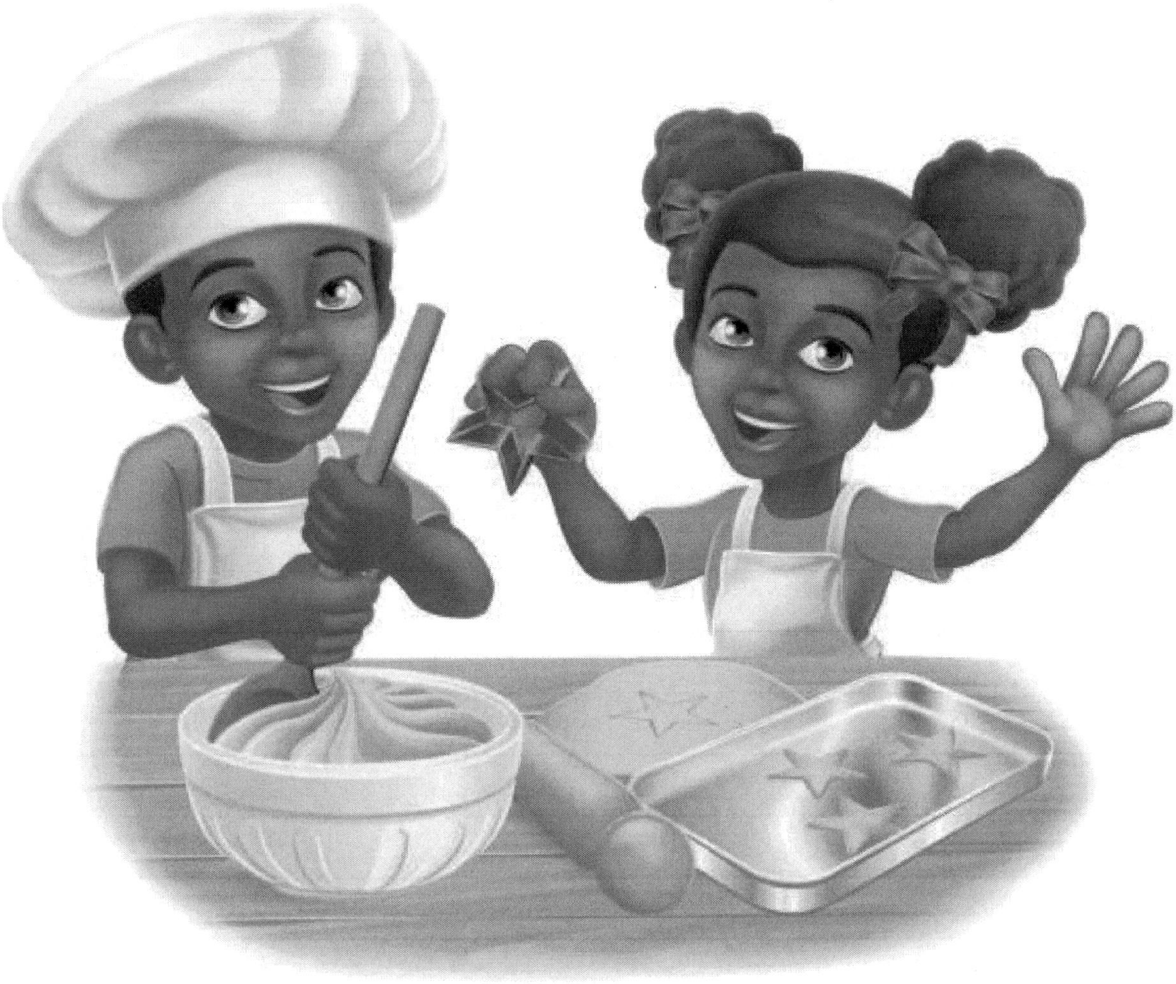

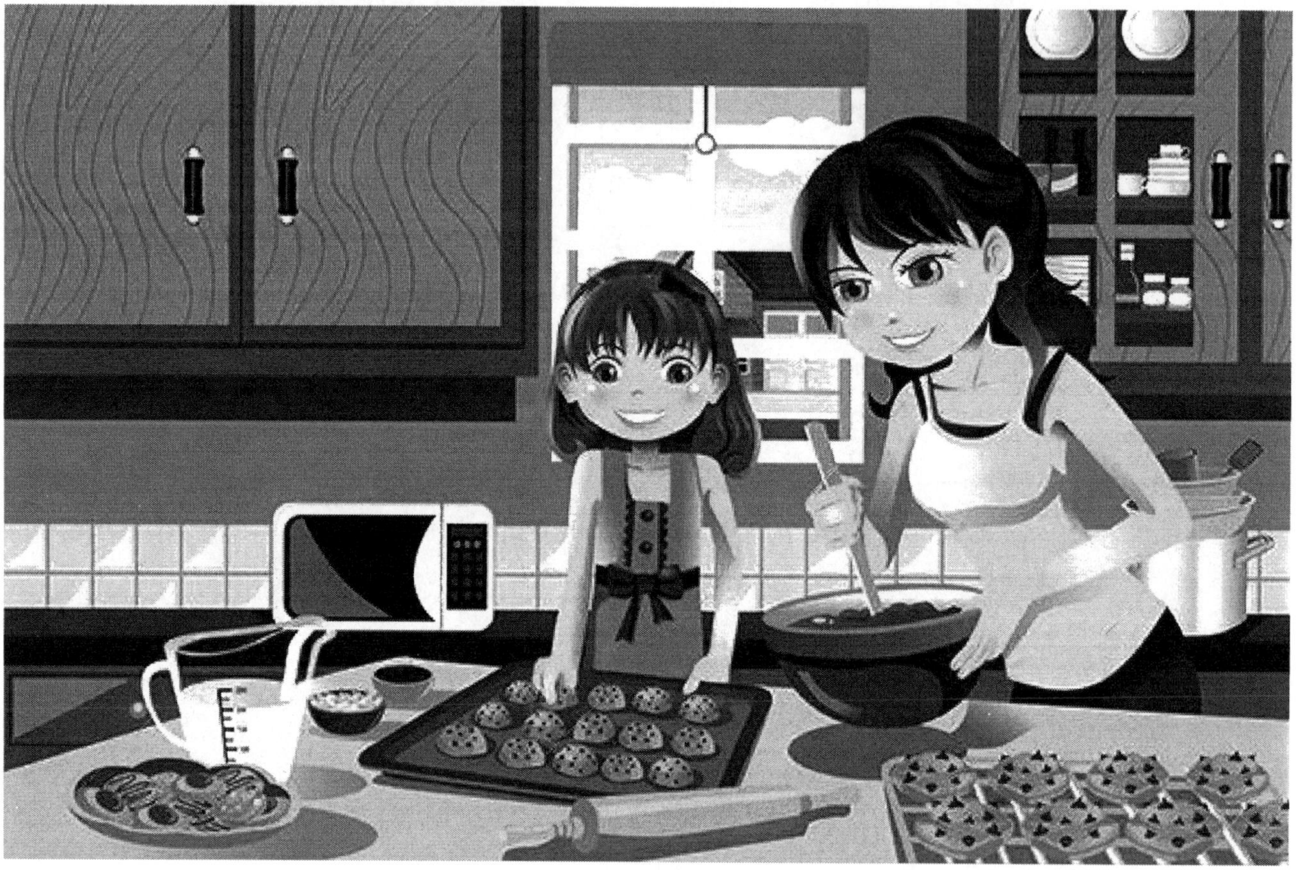

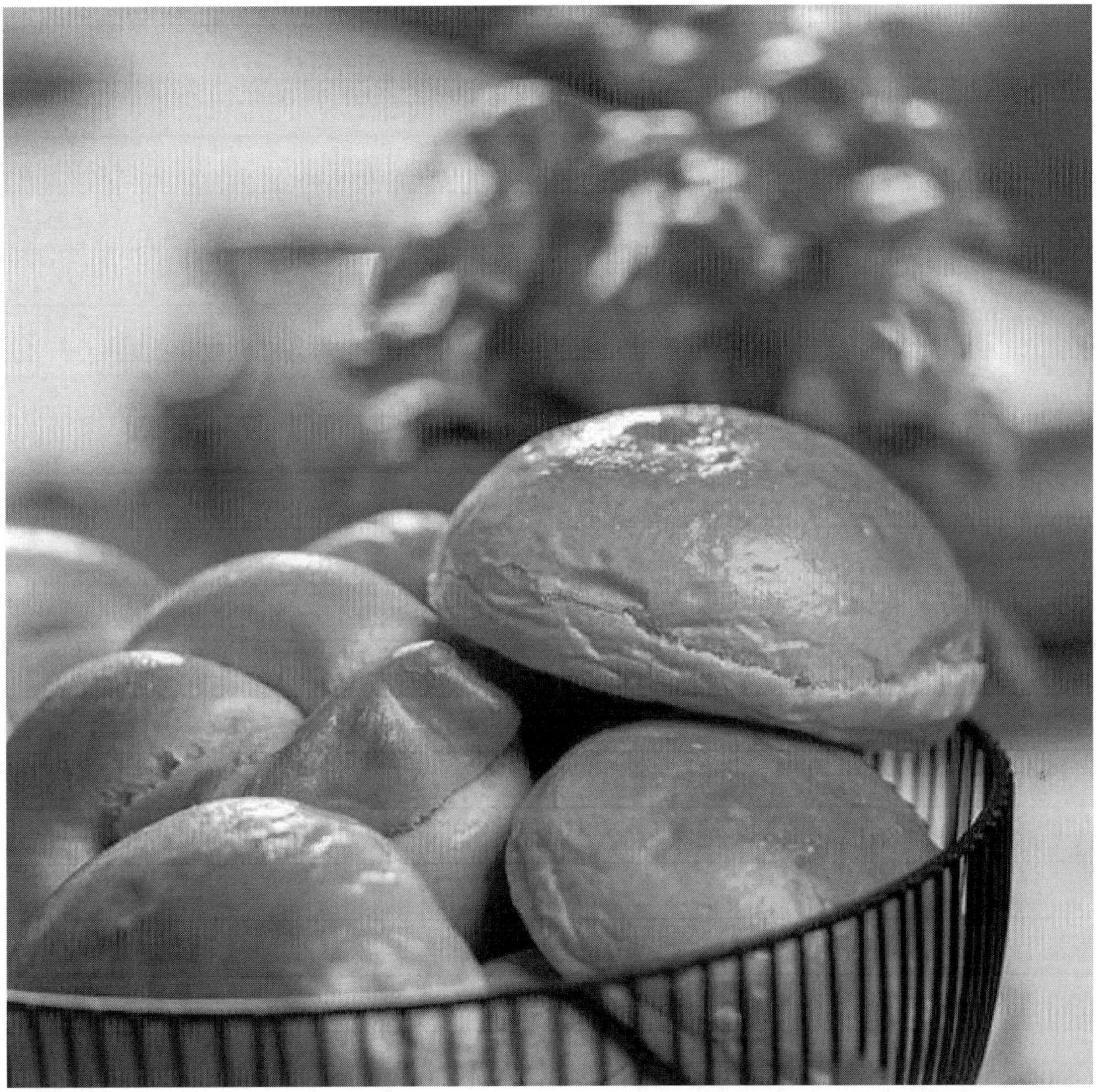

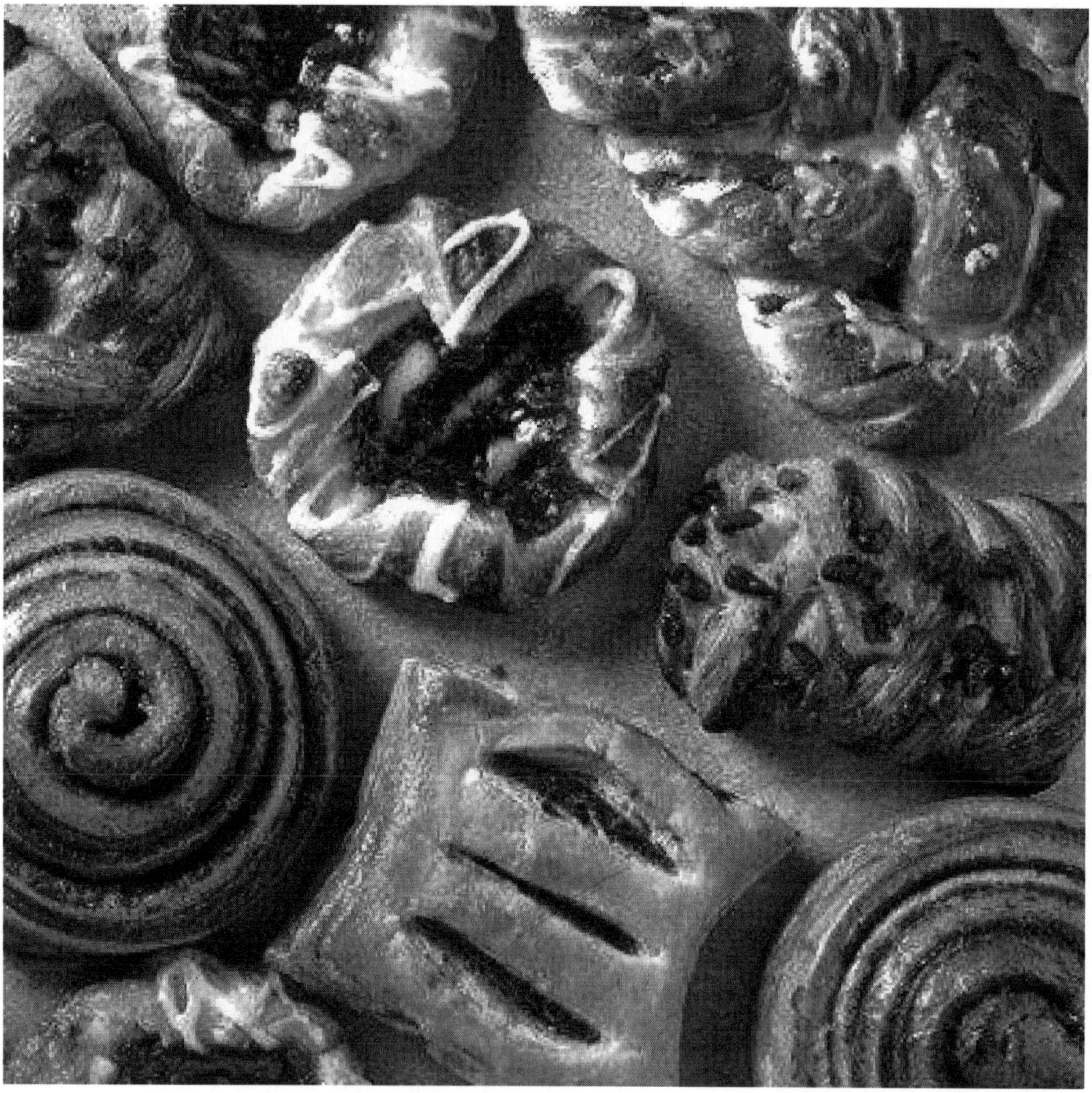

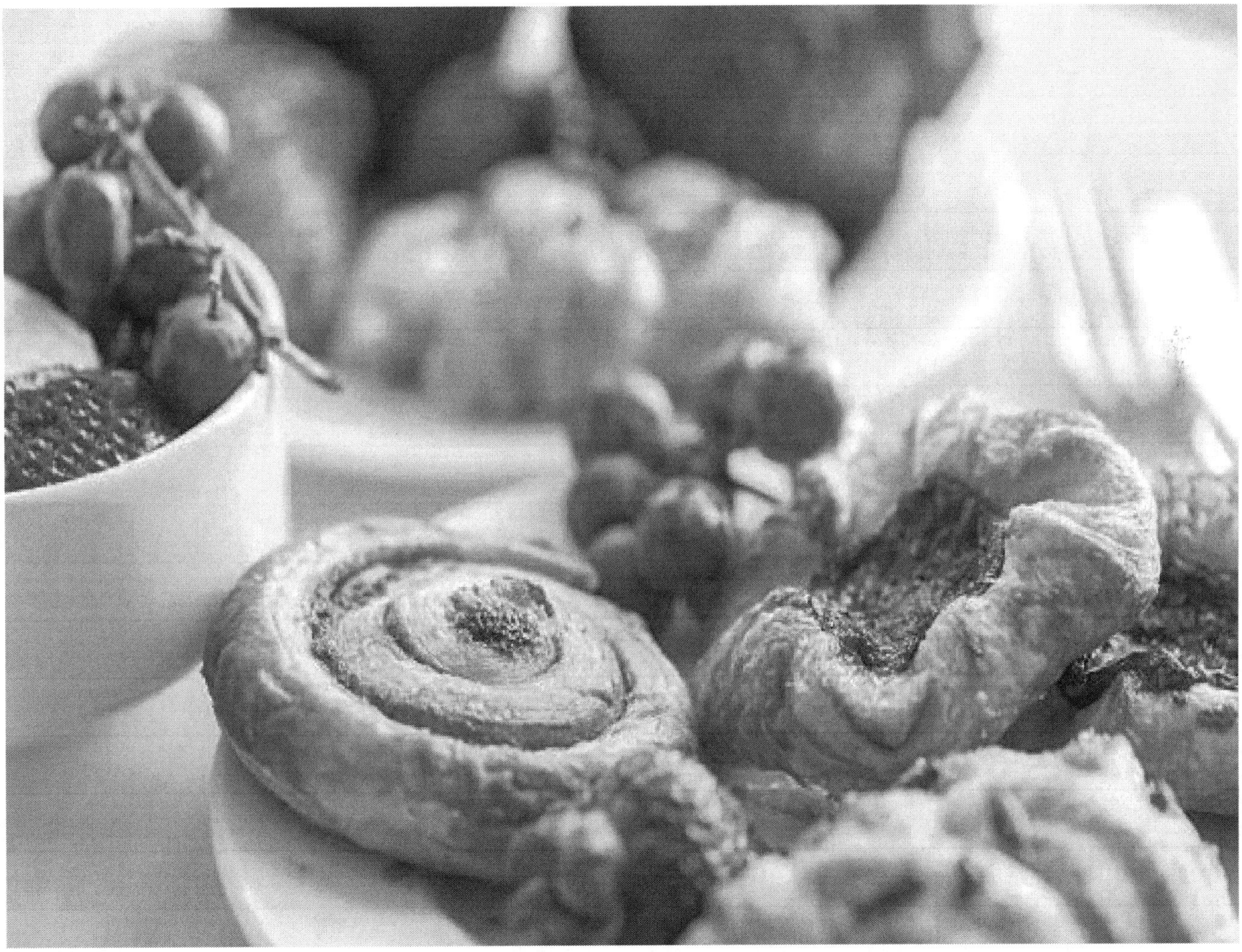

Preface

Dear Young Bakers, welcome to a world of sweetness, fun, and delicious discoveries! We are thrilled to share with you **"The Junior Baker's Cookbook: Sweet Treats and Creative Confections."** This book is like a magical recipe book, filled with treasures to help you become a baking superstar!

Do you love cookies that melt in your mouth, cupcakes that look like art, and cakes that make everyone smile?

You're in for a treat because this book is bursting with recipes just for you. Whether you're a kitchen newbie or already have a sprinkle of experience, this cookbook is here to be your friend and guide on your baking adventure.

Imagine mixing flour, sugar, and a dash of imagination to create something amazing. That's what baking is all about! But guess what? Baking is not just about following recipes – it's about having fun, being creative, and making treats that taste as good as they look.

In this book, you'll find step-by-step instructions that are easy to understand, even if you're new to baking. We've chosen simple words, colorful pictures, and fun tips to ensure you feel confident and excited in the kitchen.

You'll learn how to make classic favorites like cookies and cupcakes and dive into exciting treats like cake parfaits and more!

But wait, there's more to this book than just recipes. We'll teach you how to be safe in the kitchen, introduce you to all the cool tools and ingredients you need, and even show you how to dream up your own flavors and designs.

So, whether you're baking with your family, sharing treats with friends, or simply having a baking adventure, remember this: your kitchen is a place of magic and wonder.

It's a place where flour becomes art, and your creativity is the secret ingredient that makes everything taste even better.

Open these pages, put on your apron, and let's get baking! Every recipe you try, every frosting swirl you create, and every delightful bite you take is a step on your unique baking journey. Let's mix, measure, and make memories together.

Are you ready? Your baking adventure begins now!

Happy baking, junior chefs!

With flour-dusted high-fives and sprinkles of joy,

[Sharon D. Morgan]

Introduction

Welcome to the World of Junior Baking

Welcome to the amazing world of baking, where kids like you become super chefs in the kitchen! In this book, you'll learn how to create yummy treats to make your taste buds dance joyfully.

Whether you're baking with your family or having your own baking adventure, get ready to have fun and make delicious magic with your hands and heart.

Before we start, we'll discuss some important things to keep you safe and happy while you bake up a storm!

A Brief Note to Parents and Guardians

Hello there, wonderful grown-ups! As your kids dive into the sweet world of baking, you might have a few questions. Don't worry; we've got you covered.

This book is all about bringing smiles and tasty treats to your kitchen.

Feel free to join the fun, guide your junior bakers, and create cherished memories. We've included safety tips and helpful hints to ensure everyone has a blast.

So let's grab our aprons and create some baking magic!

Kitchen Safety Tips for Young Bakers

Safety first, junior bakers! Before baking up a storm, let's ensure you're all set to have a safe and fun time in the kitchen.

Here are some important tips to remember:

1. Wash Those Hands: Always wash your hands before baking. Clean hands make delicious treats!

2. Ask for Help: When using sharp knives, the stove, or the oven, it's a good idea to ask a grown-up for help. Safety first!

3. Apron Up: Put on an apron to keep your clothes clean and protected while you work your baking magic.

4. Read the Recipe: Before you start, read the recipe from start to finish. That way, you'll know what's coming up next.

5. Gather Ingredients: Get all your ingredients ready before you start. This way, you won't have to rush around while baking.

6. Be Careful with Hot Things: If you're using the stove, oven, or anything hot, always use oven mitts or ask for help from a grown-up.

7. Stay Organized: Keep your workspace tidy and organized. It will make baking easier and safer.

8. Taste, Not Lick: It's okay to taste your creations, but don't lick your fingers while baking. We want to keep germs out of the treats!

9. No Eating Raw Dough: Avoid eating raw dough with eggs, as tempting as it may be. Baked treats are much yummier and safer.

10. Have Fun: Baking is all about having a good time. So put on some music, wear a smile, and enjoy every moment of your baking adventure!

Remember, following these safety tips will make you a baking superstar while staying safe and sound. Happy baking, little chefs!

Essential Baking Tools and Ingredients

Let's gear up with everything you need to become a baking champion, junior bakers!

Here's a list of essential tools and ingredients that will help you create sweet masterpieces:

Baking Tools

1. Measuring Cups and Spoons: These magical tools will help you correctly measure ingredients.

2. Mixing Bowls: Different sizes of bowls for mixing and stirring your yummy creations.

3. Whisk: A whisk makes things smooth and creamy. It's like a magical wand for your batter!

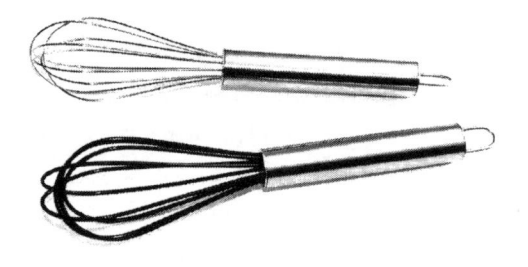

4. Wooden Spoon: Great for mixing and stirring your dough and batter.

5. Spatula: Use this to scrape every last bit of deliciousness from the bowl.

6. Baking Pans: Different shapes and sizes for cookies, cakes, and muffins.

7. Oven Mitts: Keep your hands safe from hot trays and pans.

8. Cooling Rack: Let your treats cool down and get yummy without getting soggy.

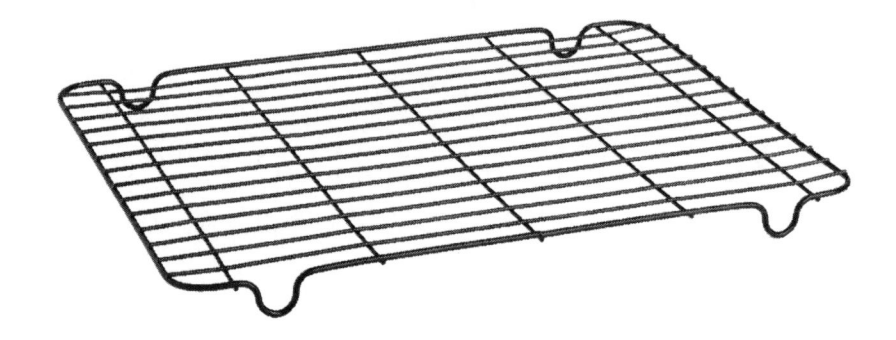

9. Rolling Pin: If you're making dough, a rolling pin helps you flatten it out.

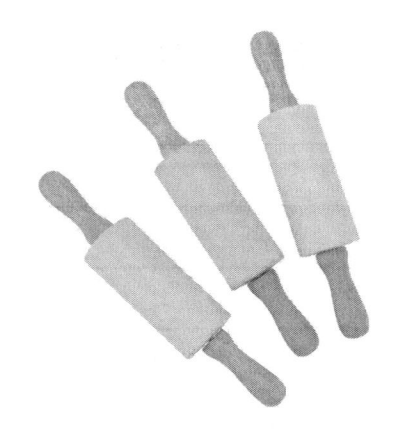

10. Cutters and Molds: Fun shapes to make your treats look extra cool.

Baking Ingredients

1. Flour: The star of baking that makes everything stick together.

2. Sugar: Adds sweetness and makes your treats yummy.

3. Butter: Creamy and delicious, it gives your baking a lovely flavor.

4. Eggs: These help your treats rise and become fluffy.

5. Baking Powder and Baking Soda: They make your treats puff up and get nice and soft.

6. Vanilla Extract: Adds a wonderful flavor to your goodies.

7. Chocolate Chips: For those delicious melty surprises in your treats.

8. Milk: Adds moisture and makes things creamy.

9. Fruits: Fresh or dried can add flavor and sweetness to your baking.

10. Sprinkles and Decorations: Make your treats look like colorful works of art!

With these awesome tools and ingredients, you're ready to dive into the world of baking and whip up some tasty treats. Get ready to have a baking blast, junior bakers!

Chapter 1: Cookie Creations

Classic Chocolate Chip Cookies

Get ready for a classic baking adventure, junior bakers! Today, we're making the all-time favorite: Chocolate Chip Cookies. These cookies are soft, chewy, and packed with gooey chocolate chips.

Here's how to make these delicious treats step by step:

Ingredients:

- 1/2 cup (1 stick) unsalted butter, softened

- 1/2 cup granulated sugar

- 1/4 cup packed brown sugar

- 1 egg

- 1 teaspoon vanilla extract

- 1 1/4 cups all-purpose flour

- 1/2 teaspoon baking soda

- 1/4 teaspoon salt

- 1 cup chocolate chips

Instructions:

1. Preheat the Oven: Ask a grown-up to help you preheat the oven to 375°F (190°C).

2. Mix the Butter and Sugars: In a mixing bowl, cream together the softened butter, granulated sugar, and brown sugar. Mix until it's smooth and creamy.

3. Add the Egg and Vanilla: Crack the egg into the bowl and add the vanilla extract. Mix everything until it's well combined.

4. Mix the Dry Ingredients: In a separate bowl, whisk together the flour, baking soda, and salt. Slowly add this dry mixture to the wet mixture in the other bowl. Mix until the ingredients come together into a dough.

5. Add the Chocolate Chips: Time for the best part! Fold the chocolate chips into the dough. You'll see the dough getting filled with chocolate goodness.

6. Shape the Cookies: Use a spoon or your hands to scoop out small portions of dough. Roll them into balls and place them on a baking sheet lined with parchment paper. Leave some space between each cookie.

7. Bake the Cookies: Pop the baking sheet into the oven and bake for 9-11 minutes or until the edges turn golden brown.

8. Cool and Enjoy: Once the cookies are baked, carefully remove the baking sheet from the oven (ask a grown-up for help). Let the cookies cool on the baking sheet for a few minutes, then transfer them to a wire rack to cool completely.

9. Time to Indulge: Now, the best part is enjoying your homemade classic chocolate chip cookies!

Please share them with family and friends, or keep them all to yourself.

Peanut Butter Blossom Cookies

Get ready for a delightful twist on cookies, junior bakers! We're making Peanut Butter Blossom Cookies, a combination of creamy peanut butter and a chocolate kiss on top.

Here's how to create these mouthwatering treats step by step:

Ingredients:

- 1/2 cup (1 stick) unsalted butter, softened
- 1/2 cup creamy peanut butter
- 1/2 cup granulated sugar
- 1/2 cup packed brown sugar
- 1 egg
- 1 teaspoon vanilla extract
- 1 3/4 cups all-purpose flour
- 1 teaspoon baking soda
- 1/2 teaspoon salt
- 36 chocolate Hershey's Kisses, unwrapped

Instructions:

1. Preheat the Oven: With a grown-up's help, preheat the oven to 375°F (190°C).

2. Blend the Butters and Sugars: In a mixing bowl, cream together the softened butter, peanut butter, granulated sugar, and brown sugar until it's light and fluffy.

3. Add the Egg and Vanilla: Crack the egg into the bowl and add the vanilla extract. Mix until everything is well combined.

4. Combine the Dry Ingredients: In another bowl, whisk together the flour, baking soda, and salt. Slowly add this dry mixture to the wet mixture and mix until it forms a smooth dough.

5. Shape the Cookies: Roll small portions of dough into balls. Roll each ball in granulated sugar and place them on a baking sheet lined with parchment paper. Leave some space between each cookie.

6. Bake and Add the Kisses: Bake the cookies for about 8-10 minutes. As soon as they come out of the oven, press a Hershey's Kiss into the center of each cookie. The cookie will crack around the edges, and the chocolate will melt slightly.

7. Cool and Enjoy: Carefully transfer the cookies to a wire rack to cool completely. Once they're cool, the chocolate kiss will be firm again, and you're ready to enjoy your Peanut Butter Blossom Cookies!

8. Spread the Joy: Share these delicious cookies with your family and friends. They'll be amazed by your baking skills!

Sugar Sprinkle Cookies

Get ready for a burst of color and sweetness, junior bakers! We're diving into the world of Sugar Sprinkle Cookies. These cookies are like tiny, edible rainbows.

Here's how you can create these colorful treats step by step:

Ingredients:

- 1/2 cup (1 stick) unsalted butter, softened
- 3/4 cup granulated sugar

- 1 egg

- 1 teaspoon vanilla extract

- 1 1/2 cups all-purpose flour

- 1/2 teaspoon baking powder

- 1/4 teaspoon salt

- Assorted colorful sprinkles

Instructions:

1. Preheat the Oven: With help from a grown-up, preheat the oven to 350°F (175°C).

2. Cream the Butter and Sugar: Cream the softened butter and granulated sugar in a mixing bowl until it's creamy and light.

3. Add the Egg and Vanilla: Crack the egg into the bowl and add the vanilla extract. Mix until everything is well combined.

4. Combine Dry Ingredients: In a separate bowl, whisk together the flour, baking powder, and salt. Slowly add this dry mixture to the wet mixture in the other bowl. Mix until it forms a smooth dough.

5. Roll in Sprinkles: Roll small portions of dough into balls. Roll each ball in colorful sprinkles, pressing them gently so they stick to the dough.

6. Flatten and Shape: Place the sprinkle-covered dough balls on a baking sheet lined with parchment paper. Gently flatten each ball with your hand or the back of a spoon.

7. Bake and Cool: Pop the baking sheet into the oven and bake for 8-10 minutes or until the edges are golden brown. Let the cookies cool on the baking sheet for a few minutes before transferring them to a wire rack to cool completely.

8. Admir and Enjoy: Look at the colorful, sprinkle-covered cookies you've made! Now it's time to enjoy these delightful treats.

9. Share the Sweetness: Share these cookies with friends, family, or anyone who needs a little sprinkle of happiness.

Oatmeal Raisin Gems

Get ready for a wholesome treat that's both chewy and delicious, junior bakers! Today, we're making Oatmeal Raisin Gems—cookies packed with the goodness of oats and the sweetness of raisins.

Let's jump right in and create these gems step by step:

Ingredients:

- 1/2 cup (1 stick) unsalted butter, softened
- 1/2 cup granulated sugar
- 1/2 cup packed brown sugar
- 1 egg
- 1 teaspoon vanilla extract
- 1 cup old-fashioned oats

- 3/4 cup all-purpose flour

- 1/2 teaspoon baking soda

- 1/2 teaspoon ground cinnamon

- 1/4 teaspoon salt

- 3/4 cup raisins

Instructions:

1. Preheat the Oven: With help from a grown-up, preheat the oven to 350°F (175°C).

2. Cream the Butter and Sugars: In a mixing bowl, cream the softened butter, granulated sugar, and brown sugar until it's creamy and smooth.

3. Add the Egg and Vanilla: Crack the egg into the bowl and add the vanilla extract. Mix everything until it's well combined.

4. Combine the Dry Ingredients: In a separate bowl, combine the oats, flour, baking soda, ground cinnamon, and salt.

5. Mix Wet and Dry Ingredients: Slowly add the dry mixture to the wet mixture and mix until it forms a dough. Then, fold in the raisins.

6. Scoop and Shape: Use a spoon or your hands to scoop out small portions of dough. Roll them into balls and place them on a baking sheet lined with parchment paper. Flatten each ball slightly with your fingers.

7. Bake and Cool: Bake the cookies for 10-12 minutes or until they turn golden brown around the edges. Let them cool on the baking sheet for a few minutes before transferring them to a wire rack to cool completely.

8. Savor the Goodness: Now, you have a batch of hearty and delicious Oatmeal Raisin Gems ready to enjoy.

9. Share the Love: These cookies are perfect for sharing with loved ones or savoring as a tasty treat whenever you need a boost.

Double Chocolate Chunk Brownie Cookies

Hold onto your aprons, junior bakers, because we're about to make a chocolate lover's dream: Double Chocolate Chunk Brownie Cookies! These cookies are perfectly blended brownie and cookie, with gooey chocolate chunks inside.

Get ready to bake up a chocolate storm with this step-by-step guide:

Ingredients:
- 1/2 cup (1 stick) unsalted butter, melted
- 1 cup granulated sugar
- 2 large eggs

- 1 teaspoon vanilla extract

- 1 cup all-purpose flour

- 1/3 cup cocoa powder

- 1/4 teaspoon baking powder

- 1/4 teaspoon salt

- 1 cup chocolate chunks or chocolate chips

Instructions:

1. Preheat the Oven: Ask a grown-up to help you preheat the oven to 350°F (175°C).

2. Mix the Wet Ingredients: Whisk the melted butter and granulated sugar in a mixing bowl until it's well combined and a bit glossy.

3. Add the Eggs and Vanilla: Crack the eggs one at a time, and add the vanilla extract. Mix everything until it's smooth and creamy.

4. Combine the Dry Ingredients: In a separate bowl, whisk together the flour, cocoa powder, baking powder, and salt.

5. Mix Wet and Dry Ingredients: Slowly add the dry mixture to the wet mixture and mix until it forms a thick, chocolaty dough.

6. Add the Chocolate Chunks: Fold the chocolate chunks or chips. The more, the merrier!

7. Shape the Cookies: Scoop small portions of dough and place them on a baking sheet lined with parchment paper. Leave some space between each cookie.

8. Bake and Enjoy: Add the baking sheet to the oven and bake for 10-12 minutes. When you take them out, the cookies will be slightly soft in the center.

9. Cool and Savor: Let the cookies cool on the baking sheet for a few minutes before transferring them to a wire rack to cool completely. This helps them become chewy and amazing.

10. Chocoholic Delight: Sink your teeth into these double chocolate chunk brownie cookies. The gooey chocolate bits will make you smile!

11. Share the Chocolate Love: Share these cookies with fellow chocolate enthusiasts, or keep them all to yourself for a private chocolate party!

Chapter 2: Cupcake Delights

Vanilla Cupcakes with Buttercream Frosting

Get ready to bake and frost some tasty treats, junior bakers! We're making Vanilla Cupcakes with Buttercream Frosting—a delicious combination that's as fun to make as it is to eat.

Let's get started step by step:

Ingredients for Cupcakes:

- 1/2 cup (1 stick) unsalted butter, softened

- 1/2 cup granulated sugar

- 2 eggs

- 1 teaspoon vanilla extract

- 1 cup all-purpose flour

- 1 1/2 teaspoons baking powder

- 1/4 teaspoon salt

- 1/2 cup milk

Ingredients for Buttercream Frosting:

- 1/2 cup (1 stick) unsalted butter, softened

- 2 cups powdered sugar

- 1 teaspoon vanilla extract

- 2-3 tablespoons milk

Instructions:

For the Cupcakes:

1. Preheat the Oven: Ask a grown-up to help you preheat the oven to 350°F (175°C).

2. Mix the Wet Ingredients: Mix the softened butter and granulated sugar in a mixing bowl until it's smooth and creamy.

3. Add the Eggs and Vanilla: Crack the eggs one at a time, and add the vanilla extract. Mix everything until it's well combined.

4. Combine the Dry Ingredients: In a separate bowl, mix the flour, baking powder, and salt. Slowly add this mixture to the wet mixture, alternating with the milk. Mix until it's a smooth batter.

5. Fill the Cupcake Liners: Place cupcake liners in a muffin tin. Scoop the batter into each liner, filling them about two-thirds full.

6. Bake the Cupcakes: With a grown-up's help, bake the cupcakes for about 15-18 minutes or until a toothpick inserted in the center comes out clean.

7. Cool the Cupcakes: Let the cupcakes cool in the muffin tin for a few minutes, then transfer them to a wire rack to cool completely.

For the Buttercream Frosting:

1. Mix the Butter and Sugar: In a mixing bowl, beat the softened butter until it's creamy. Gradually add the powdered sugar while mixing.

2. Add Vanilla and Milk: Mix in the vanilla extract. Slowly add the milk, one tablespoon at a time, until you have a smooth and creamy frosting.

3. Frost the Cupcakes: Once the cupcakes are completely cool, use a butter knife or a piping bag to spread or pipe the buttercream frosting onto the cupcakes. You can get creative with your designs!

4. Enjoy Your Creations: Now you have delightful Vanilla Cupcakes with Buttercream Frosting ready to be enjoyed. Yum!

Chocolate Fudge Cupcakes

Time to create chocolaty perfection, junior bakers! We're making Chocolate Fudge Cupcakes—rich and irresistible treats that will make your taste buds dance.

Let's get started step by step:

Ingredients for Cupcakes:

- 1/2 cup (1 stick) unsalted butter, softened

- 1 cup granulated sugar

- 2 eggs

- 1 teaspoon vanilla extract

- 1 cup all-purpose flour

- 1/2 cup cocoa powder

- 1 teaspoon baking powder

- 1/2 teaspoon baking soda

- 1/4 teaspoon salt

- 3/4 cup milk

Ingredients for Chocolate Fudge Frosting:

- 1/2 cup (1 stick) unsalted butter, softened

- 2 cups powdered sugar

- 1/4 cup cocoa powder

- 1/4 cup milk

- 1 teaspoon vanilla extract

Instructions:

For the Cupcakes:

1. Preheat the Oven: With help from a grown-up, preheat the oven to 350°F (175°C).

2. Mix the Wet Ingredients: In a mixing bowl, cream the softened butter and granulated sugar until smooth and creamy.

3. Add the Eggs and Vanilla: Crack the eggs one at a time, and add the vanilla extract. Mix everything until it's well combined.

4. Combine the Dry Ingredients: In a separate bowl, whisk together the flour, cocoa powder, baking powder, baking soda, and salt.

5. Alternate Wet and Dry Ingredients: Gradually add the dry mixture and milk to the wet mixture, starting and ending with the dry ingredients. Mix until you have a smooth and chocolaty batter.

6. Fill the Cupcake Liners: Line a muffin tin with cupcake liners. Spoon the batter into each liner, filling them about two-thirds full.

7. Bake the Cupcakes: With a grown-up's help, bake the cupcakes for about 18-20 minutes or until a toothpick inserted in the center comes out clean.

Let them cool in the muffin tin for a few minutes before transferring them to a wire rack to cool completely.

For the Chocolate Fudge Frosting:

1. Mix the Butter and Sugar: In a mixing bowl, beat the softened butter until it's creamy. Gradually add the powdered sugar and cocoa powder, mixing until well combined.

2. Add Milk and Vanilla: Slowly add the milk and vanilla extract while mixing. Continue mixing until you have a luscious and velvety chocolate fudge frosting.

3. Frost the Cupcakes: Once the cupcakes are completely cooled, generously spread or pipe the chocolate fudge frosting onto each cupcake.

4. Indulge and Delight: Congratulations! You've made delicious Chocolate Fudge Cupcakes that will delight everyone who tries them.

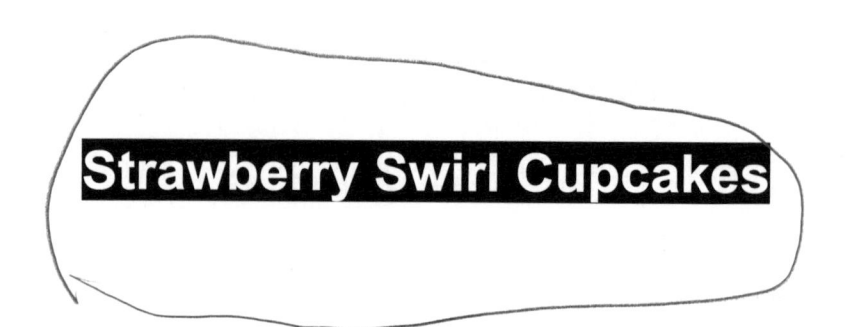

Strawberry Swirl Cupcakes

Get ready to add a fruity twist to your cupcakes, junior bakers! Today, we're making Strawberry Swirl Cupcakes—delicious treats with a swirl of sweet strawberry goodness.

Let's dive into this fruity baking adventure step by step:

Ingredients for Cupcakes:

- 1/2 cup (1 stick) unsalted butter, softened
- 1 cup granulated sugar
- 2 eggs
- 1 teaspoon vanilla extract
- 1 1/2 cups all-purpose flour
- 1 1/2 teaspoons baking powder
- 1/4 teaspoon salt
- 1/2 cup milk

Ingredients for Strawberry Swirl:

- 1/2 cup fresh strawberries, hulled and pureed
- 2 tablespoons granulated sugar

Ingredients for Strawberry Cream Cheese Frosting:

- 1/2 cup (1 stick) unsalted butter, softened
- 4 ounces cream cheese, softened
- 2 cups powdered sugar
- 1/2 teaspoon vanilla extract
- 2 tablespoons strawberry puree (from earlier)

Instructions:

For the Cupcakes:

1. Preheat the Oven: Ask a grown-up to help you preheat the oven to 350°F (175°C).

2. Mix the Wet Ingredients: In a mixing bowl, cream the softened butter and granulated sugar until it's creamy and smooth.

3. Add the Eggs and Vanilla: Crack the eggs one at a time, and add the vanilla extract. Mix everything until it's well combined.

4. Combine the Dry Ingredients: In a separate bowl, whisk together the flour, baking powder, and salt.

5. Alternate Wet and Dry Ingredients: Gradually add the dry mixture and milk to the wet mixture, starting and ending with the dry ingredients. Mix until you have a smooth batter.

6. Fill the Cupcake Liners: Line a muffin tin with cupcake liners. Spoon the batter into each liner, filling them about two-thirds full.

7. Make the Strawberry Swirl: Mix the strawberry puree and granulated sugar in a small bowl until well combined.

8. Add the Swirl: Drop a small spoonful of the strawberry mixture onto the batter in each cupcake liner. Use a toothpick to gently swirl the strawberry into the batter to create a marbled effect.

9. Bake and Cool: With a grown-up's help, bake the cupcakes for about 18-20 minutes. Let them cool in the muffin tin for a few minutes before transferring them to a wire rack to cool completely.

For the Strawberry Cream Cheese Frosting:

1. Mix Butter and Cream Cheese: In a mixing bowl, beat the softened butter and cream cheese until smooth and creamy.

2. Add Sugar and Vanilla: Gradually add the powdered sugar and vanilla extract while mixing.

3. Add Strawberry Puree: Mix in the strawberry puree until the frosting is light and fluffy.

4. Frost the Cupcakes: Once the cupcakes are completely cooled, generously spread or pipe the strawberry cream cheese frosting onto each cupcake.

5. Enjoy the Sweetness: Now you have beautiful and tasty Strawberry Swirl Cupcakes ready to be enjoyed!

Funfetti Surprise Cupcakes

Get ready for a cupcake full of colorful surprises, junior bakers! Today, we're making Funfetti Surprise Cupcakes—adorable treats with hidden surprises.

Let's get started on this colorful baking adventure step by step:

Ingredients for Cupcakes:

- 1/2 cup (1 stick) unsalted butter, softened

- 1 cup granulated sugar

- 2 eggs

- 1 teaspoon vanilla extract

- 1 1/2 cups all-purpose flour

- 1 1/2 teaspoons baking powder

- 1/4 teaspoon salt

- 1/2 cup milk

- 1/4 cup rainbow sprinkles (for the batter)

Ingredients for Surprise Filling:

- Your favorite candies or mini chocolate chips

Ingredients for Vanilla Buttercream Frosting:

- 1/2 cup (1 stick) unsalted butter, softened

- 2 cups powdered sugar

- 1 teaspoon vanilla extract

- 2-3 tablespoons milk

- Extra rainbow sprinkles (for decorating)

Instructions:

For the Cupcakes:

1. Preheat the Oven: With help from a grown-up, preheat the oven to 350°F (175°C).

2. Mix the Wet Ingredients: In a mixing bowl, cream the softened butter and granulated sugar until it's creamy and smooth.

3. Add the Eggs and Vanilla: Crack the eggs one at a time, and add the vanilla extract. Mix everything until it's well combined.

4. Combine the Dry Ingredients: In a separate bowl, whisk together the flour, baking powder, and salt.

5. Alternate Wet and Dry Ingredients: Gradually add the dry mixture and milk to the wet mixture, starting and ending with the dry ingredients. Mix until you have a smooth batter.

6. Add the Funfetti: Gently fold in the rainbow sprinkles. They'll bring a burst of color to your cupcakes!

7. Fill the Cupcake Liners: Line a muffin tin with cupcake liners. Spoon a small batter into each liner, just enough to cover the bottom.

8. Add the Surprise: Drop a surprise candy or mini chocolate chips into the center of each cupcake, on top of the batter.

9. Finish Filling the Cupcakes: Cover the candy or chips with more batter until each cupcake liner is about two-thirds full.

10. Bake and Cool: With a grown-up's help, bake the cupcakes for about 18-20 minutes. Let them cool in the muffin tin for a few minutes before transferring them to a wire rack to cool completely.

For the Vanilla Buttercream Frosting:

1. Mix Butter and Sugar: In a mixing bowl, beat the softened butter until it's creamy. Gradually add the powdered sugar, mixing until well combined.

2. Add Vanilla and Milk: Mix in the vanilla extract. Slowly add the milk, one tablespoon at a time, while mixing. Continue mixing until the frosting is smooth and fluffy.

3. Frost the Cupcakes: Once the cupcakes are completely cooled, generously spread or pipe the vanilla buttercream frosting onto each cupcake.

4. Sprinkle the Joy: Decorate the cupcakes with rainbow sprinkles for extra fun!

5. Uncover the Surprise: Now you have delightful Funfetti Surprise Cupcakes ready to bring smiles and surprises to everyone.

Lemon Zest Cupcakes with Creamy Lemon Frosting

Get ready to add a zesty twist to your cupcakes, junior bakers! Today, we're making Lemon Zest Cupcakes with Creamy Lemon Frosting—delightful treats with citrusy flavor.

Let's jump into this tangy and delicious baking adventure step by step:

Ingredients for Cupcakes:

- 1/2 cup (1 stick) unsalted butter, softened

- 1 cup granulated sugar

- 2 eggs

- 1 teaspoon vanilla extract

- Zest of 1 lemon

- 1 1/2 cups all-purpose flour

- 1 1/2 teaspoons baking powder

- 1/4 teaspoon salt

- 1/2 cup milk

- 2 tablespoons fresh lemon juice

Ingredients for Creamy Lemon Frosting:

- 1/2 cup (1 stick) unsalted butter, softened

- 2 cups powdered sugar

- Zest of 1 lemon

- 2 tablespoons fresh lemon juice

- 1-2 tablespoons milk (if needed)

Instructions:

For the Cupcakes:

1. Preheat the Oven: With help from a grown-up, preheat the oven to 350°F (175°C).

2. Mix the Wet Ingredients: In a mixing bowl, cream the softened butter and granulated sugar until it's creamy and smooth.

3. Add the Eggs and Vanilla: Crack the eggs one at a time, and add the vanilla extract. Mix everything until it's well combined.

4. Add Lemon Zest: Grate the zest of one lemon and add it to the batter. Mix it in to infuse the cupcakes with zesty flavor.

5. Combine the Dry Ingredients: In a separate bowl, whisk together the flour, baking powder, and salt.

6. Alternate Wet and Dry Ingredients: Gradually add the dry mixture and milk to the wet mixture, starting and ending with the dry ingredients. Mix until you have a smooth batter.

7. Add Lemon Juice: Mix in the fresh lemon juice. The batter will have a lovely lemony aroma and taste.

8. Fill the Cupcake Liners: Line a muffin tin with cupcake liners. Spoon the batter into each liner, filling them about two-thirds full.

9. Bake and Cool: With a grown-up's help, bake the cupcakes for about 18-20 minutes. Let them cool in the muffin tin for a few minutes before transferring them to a wire rack to cool completely.

For the Creamy Lemon Frosting:

1. Mix Butter and Sugar: In a mixing bowl, beat the softened butter until it's creamy. Gradually add the powdered sugar, mixing until well combined.

2. Add Lemon Zest and Juice: Mix in the lemon zest and fresh lemon juice. The frosting will be zingy and delightful.

3. Adjust Consistency: If the frosting is too thick, add 1-2 tablespoons of milk and mix until you achieve a creamy and spreadable consistency.

4. Frost the Cupcakes: Once the cupcakes are completely cooled, generously spread or pipe the creamy lemon frosting onto each cupcake.

5. Zest Up Your Treats: Top each cupcake with a sprinkle of lemon zest for an extra burst of lemon flavor.

6. Savor the Zesty Goodness: Now you have beautifully zesty Lemon Zest Cupcakes with Creamy Lemon Frosting ready to be enjoyed!

Chapter 3: Cake Magic

Rainbow Layer Cake with Whipped Cream Frosting

Get ready to create a dazzling dessert masterpiece, junior bakers! Today, we're making a Rainbow Layer Cake with Whipped Cream Frosting—a colorful and dreamy treat that's as enchanting to look at as it is to eat.

Let's dive into this rainbow-filled baking adventure step by step:

Ingredients for the Cake:

- 2 1/2 cups all-purpose flour
- 2 1/2 teaspoons baking powder
- 1/2 teaspoon salt
- 1 1/4 cups unsalted butter, softened
- 2 cups granulated sugar
- 4 large eggs
- 1 teaspoon vanilla extract
- 1 cup milk
- Food coloring in various colors (red, orange, yellow, green, blue, purple)

Ingredients for Whipped Cream Frosting:

- 2 cups heavy whipping cream
- 1/4 cup powdered sugar

- 1 teaspoon vanilla extract

Instructions:

For the Cake:

1. Preheat the Oven: With help from a grown-up, preheat the oven to 350°F (175°C). Grease and line three 8-inch round cake pans with parchment paper.

2. Mix the Dry Ingredients: In a bowl, whisk together the flour, baking powder, and salt.

3. Cream Butter and Sugar: In a separate large bowl, cream the softened butter and granulated sugar until it's light and fluffy.

4. Add Eggs and Vanilla: Crack the eggs one at a time, and add the vanilla extract. Mix until well combined.

5. Alternate Wet and Dry Ingredients: Gradually add the dry mixture and milk to the wet mixture, starting and ending with the dry ingredients. Mix until you have a smooth batter.

6. Divide and Color: Divide the batter equally into six smaller bowls. Add different food coloring to each bowl to create rainbow colors.

7. Layer the Colors: Starting with one color, spoon a small amount of batter into the center of the first cake pan. Use a spatula to spread it gently to the edges. Repeat this process with the other colors, stacking the layers on each other.

8. Bake the Cake: With a grown-up's help, bake the cake layers for about 20-25 minutes or until a toothpick inserted in the center comes out clean. Let them cool in the pans for a few minutes before transferring them to a wire rack to cool completely.

For the Whipped Cream Frosting:

1. Chill the Bowl and Whisk: Place the mixing bowl and whisk attachment in the refrigerator for about 15 minutes to chill.

2. Whip the Cream: Pour the heavy whipping cream into the chilled bowl and start beating on medium speed. Gradually add the powdered sugar and vanilla extract. Continue beating until the cream holds stiff peaks.

Assemble the Rainbow Layer Cake:

1. Level the Cake Layers: If the cake layers have domed tops, use a serrated knife to level them gently.

2. Frost the Layers: Place one cake layer on a serving plate. Spread a generous layer of whipped cream frosting over the top. Repeat with the other layers.

3. Frost the Sides: Use the remaining whipped cream frosting to frost the sides of the cake. Smooth the frosting using an offset spatula.

4. Decorate: Get creative with additional rainbow sprinkles, colorful decorations, or even some extra whipped cream dollops on top.

5. Slice and Enjoy: Now you have a stunning Rainbow Layer Cake with Whipped Cream Frosting ready to be enjoyed slice by colorful slice!

Marble Cake with Chocolate Ganache

Get ready to create a beautiful and delicious Marble Cake with Chocolate Ganache, junior bakers! This cake combines two delightful flavors and a rich ganache topping.

Let's dive into this delightful baking adventure step by step:

Ingredients for the Cake:

- 2 1/2 cups all-purpose flour

- 2 1/2 teaspoons baking powder

- 1/2 teaspoon salt

- 1 1/4 cups unsalted butter, softened

- 2 cups granulated sugar

- 4 large eggs

- 1 teaspoon vanilla extract

- 1 cup milk

- 1/4 cup unsweetened cocoa powder

Ingredients for Chocolate Ganache:

- 1 cup heavy cream

- 8 ounces semi-sweet chocolate, chopped

Instructions:

For the Cake:

1. Preheat the Oven: With help from a grown-up, preheat the oven to 350°F (175°C). Grease and line two 8-inch round cake pans with parchment paper.

2. Mix the Dry Ingredients: In a bowl, whisk together the flour, baking powder, and salt.

3. Cream Butter and Sugar: In a separate large bowl, cream the softened butter and granulated sugar until it's light and fluffy.

4. Add Eggs and Vanilla: Crack the eggs one at a time, and add the vanilla extract. Mix until well combined.

5. Alternate Wet and Dry Ingredients: Gradually add the dry mixture and milk to the wet mixture, starting and ending with the dry ingredients. Mix until you have a smooth batter.

6. Divide and Marble: Divide the batter equally into two bowls. Sift in the cocoa powder in one bowl and mix until fully incorporated.

7. Marble the Batter: Spoon a portion into one cake pan, starting with the vanilla batter. Then, spoon a portion of the chocolate batter on top. Continue layering the batters alternately until both pans are filled.

Use a skewer or a knife to swirl the batters together to create a marbled effect gently.

8. Bake the Cake: With a grown-up's help, bake the cake layers for about 25-30 minutes or until a toothpick inserted in the center comes out clean. Let them cool in the pans for a few minutes before transferring them to a wire rack to cool completely.

For the Chocolate Ganache:

1. Chop the Chocolate: Place the chopped semi-sweet chocolate in a heatproof bowl.

2. Heat the Cream: Heat the heavy cream in a saucepan until it's just about to boil. Pour the hot cream over the chopped chocolate.

3. Create the Ganache: Let the cream and chocolate sit for a minute, then gently whisk until the chocolate is completely melted and the mixture is smooth and glossy.

Assemble the Marble Cake:

1. Level the Cake Layers: If the cake layers have domed tops, use a serrated knife to level them gently.

2. Spread Ganache: Place one cake layer on a serving plate. Spread a layer of chocolate ganache over the top. Repeat with the other layer.

3. Ganache Drizzle: Pour some of the ganache over the top of the cake and let it drip down the sides for a beautiful drizzle effect.

4. Set and Enjoy: Allow the ganache to set slightly before slicing and enjoying your Marble Cake with Chocolate Ganache.

Red Velvet Cake with Cream Cheese Frosting

Get ready to bake a classic favorite, junior bakers! Today, we're making a Red Velvet Cake with Cream Cheese Frosting—a perfect combination of rich flavor and creamy sweetness.

Let's dive into this delightful baking adventure step by step:

Ingredients for the Cake:
- 2 1/2 cups all-purpose flour
- 1 1/2 cups granulated sugar
- 1 teaspoon baking powder
- 1 teaspoon baking soda
- 1 teaspoon cocoa powder
- 1/2 teaspoon salt
- 1 1/2 cups vegetable oil
- 1 cup buttermilk
- 2 large eggs
- 2 teaspoons vanilla extract
- 1-ounce red food coloring (about two tablespoons)

Ingredients for Cream Cheese Frosting:

- 1/2 cup (1 stick) unsalted butter, softened

- 8 ounces cream cheese, softened

- 4 cups powdered sugar

- 1 teaspoon vanilla extract

Instructions:

For the Cake:

1. Preheat the Oven: With help from a grown-up, preheat the oven to 350°F (175°C). Grease and flour two 9-inch round cake pans.

2. Mix the Dry Ingredients: In a bowl, whisk together the flour, granulated sugar, baking powder, baking soda, cocoa powder, and salt.

3. Mix the Wet Ingredients: In a separate bowl, whisk together the vegetable oil, buttermilk, eggs, vanilla extract, and red food coloring until well combined.

4. Combine Wet and Dry Ingredients: Gradually add the wet mixture to the dry mixture until smooth and well combined.

5. Divide and Bake: Divide the batter equally between the prepared cake pans. Bake for about 25-30 minutes or until a toothpick inserted in the center comes out clean.

Let the cakes cool in the pans for a few minutes before transferring them to a wire rack to cool completely.

For the Cream Cheese Frosting:

1. Mix Butter and Cream Cheese: In a mixing bowl, beat the softened butter and cream cheese until smooth and creamy.

2. Add Sugar and Vanilla: Gradually add the powdered sugar and vanilla extract while mixing.

Assemble the Red Velvet Cake:

1. Level the Cake Layers: If the cake layers have domed tops, use a serrated knife to level them gently.

2. Frost the Layers: Place one cake layer on a serving plate. Spread a generous layer of cream cheese frosting over the top. Repeat with the other layer.

3. Frost the Sides: Use the remaining cream cheese frosting to frost the sides of the cake. You can leave the sides semi-naked for a rustic look or frost them completely for a smoother finish.

4. Decorate: If desired, decorate the cake with red velvet cake crumbs or additional frosting swirls.

5. Slice and Enjoy: Now you have a luscious Red Velvet Cake with Cream Cheese Frosting ready to be enjoyed slice by delicious slice!

Raspberry Almond Cake

Get ready to bake a delightful fruity treat, junior bakers! Today, we're making a Raspberry Almond Cake—a delicious combination of tangy raspberries and nutty almonds.

Let's dive into this delightful baking adventure step by step:

Ingredients for the Cake:

- 1 1/2 cups all-purpose flour

- 1 1/2 teaspoons baking powder

- 1/4 teaspoon salt

- 1/2 cup (1 stick) unsalted butter, softened

- 1 cup granulated sugar

- 2 large eggs

- 1 teaspoon almond extract

- 1/2 cup milk

- 1 1/2 cups fresh raspberries

Ingredients for Almond Glaze:

- 1 cup powdered sugar

- 2 tablespoons milk

- 1/2 teaspoon almond extract

- Sliced almonds (for topping)

Instructions:

For the Cake:

1. Preheat the Oven: With help from a grown-up, preheat the oven to 350°F (175°C). Grease and flour a 9-inch round cake pan.

2. Mix the Dry Ingredients: In a bowl, whisk together the flour, baking powder, and salt.

3. Cream Butter and Sugar: In a separate large bowl, cream the softened butter and granulated sugar until it's light and fluffy.

4. Add Eggs and Almond Extract: Crack the eggs one at a time and add the almond extract. Mix until well combined.

5. Alternate Wet and Dry Ingredients: Gradually add the dry mixture and milk to the wet mixture, starting and ending with the dry ingredients. Mix until you have a smooth batter.

6. Fold in Raspberries: Gently fold in the fresh raspberries. The batter will turn a beautiful pink color!

7. Bake the Cake: With a grown-up's help, pour the batter into the prepared cake pan and smooth the top.

Bake for about 35-40 minutes or until a toothpick inserted in the center comes out clean. Let the cake cool in the pan for a few minutes before transferring it to a wire rack to cool completely.

For the Almond Glaze:

1. Mix Glaze Ingredients: In a bowl, whisk together the powdered sugar, milk, and almond extract until you have a smooth and pourable glaze.

Assemble the Raspberry Almond Cake:

1. Glaze the Cake: Place the cooled cake on a serving plate. Drizzle the almond glaze over the top, allowing it to drip down the sides.

2. Almond Crunch: Sprinkle sliced almonds on top of the glaze to add a delightful crunch and nutty flavor.

3. Slice and Enjoy: Now you have a delicious Raspberry Almond Cake ready to be enjoyed slice by juice!

Carrot Cake with Creamy Maple Frosting

Get ready to bake a moist and flavorful treat, junior bakers! Today, we're making a Carrot Cake with Creamy Maple Frosting—a perfect blend of sweetness and warmth.

Let's dive into this delightful baking adventure step by step:

Ingredients for the Carrot Cake:
- 2 cups all-purpose flour
- 2 teaspoons baking powder
- 1 1/2 teaspoons baking soda
- 1 teaspoon ground cinnamon
- 1/2 teaspoon ground nutmeg
- 1/2 teaspoon salt
- 1 cup granulated sugar
- 1 cup vegetable oil
- 4 large eggs
- 2 cups finely grated carrots
- 1/2 cup crushed pineapple, drained
- 1/2 cup chopped walnuts or pecans (optional)

Ingredients for Creamy Maple Frosting:

- 1/2 cup (1 stick) unsalted butter, softened

- 8 ounces cream cheese, softened

- 4 cups powdered sugar

- 1 teaspoon vanilla extract

- 2-3 tablespoons pure maple syrup

Instructions:

For the Carrot Cake:

1. Preheat the Oven: With help from a grown-up, preheat the oven to 350°F (175°C). Grease and flour two 9-inch round cake pans.

2. Mix the Dry Ingredients: In a bowl, whisk together the flour, baking powder, baking soda, cinnamon, nutmeg, and salt.

3. Mix the Wet Ingredients: Whisk the granulated sugar and vegetable oil in a separate large bowl until well combined. Add the eggs one at a time, mixing well after each addition.

4. Combine Wet and Dry Ingredients: Gradually add the dry mixture to the wet mixture until just combined.

5. Fold in Carrots, Pineapple, and Nuts: Gently fold in the grated carrots, crushed pineapple, and chopped nuts (if using).

6. Bake the Cake: With a grown-up's help, divide the batter equally between the prepared cake pans. Bake for about 30-35 minutes or until a toothpick inserted in the center comes out clean. Let the cakes cool in the pans for a few minutes before transferring them to a wire rack to cool completely.

For the Creamy Maple Frosting:

1. Mix Butter and Cream Cheese: In a mixing bowl, beat the softened butter and cream cheese until smooth and creamy.

2. Add Sugar and Vanilla: Gradually add the powdered sugar and vanilla extract while mixing.

3. Add Maple Syrup: Mix in the pure maple syrup until the frosting is smooth and has a delightful hint of maple flavor.

Assemble the Carrot Cake:

1. Level the Cake Layers: If the cake layers have domed tops, use a serrated knife to level them gently.

2. Frost the Layers: Place one cake layer on a serving plate. Spread a generous layer of creamy maple frosting over the top. Repeat with the other layer.

3. Frost the Sides: Use the remaining creamy maple frosting to frost the sides of the cake. You can leave the sides semi-naked for a rustic look or frost them completely for a smoother finish.

4. Decorate: If desired, decorate the cake with additional chopped nuts, grated carrots, or a drizzle of maple syrup.

5. Slice and Enjoy: Now you have a delightful Carrot Cake with Creamy Maple Frosting ready to be enjoyed slice by flavorful slice!

Chapter 4: Sweet Breads and Muffins

Banana Nut Bread

Get ready to bake a classic comfort treat, junior bakers! Today, we're making Banana Nut Bread—a moist and flavorful bread perfect for snacking.

Let's dive into this delicious baking adventure step by step:

Ingredients:
- 2 to 3 ripe bananas, mashed
- 1/3 cup melted butter
- 1 teaspoon baking soda
- Pinch of salt
- 3/4 cup granulated sugar
- 1 large egg, beaten
- 1 teaspoon vanilla extract
- 1 1/2 cups all-purpose flour
- 1/2 cup chopped nuts (walnuts or pecans)

Instructions:

1. Preheat the Oven: With help from a grown-up, preheat the oven to 350°F (175°C). Grease a 4x8-inch loaf pan.

2. Mash the Bananas: In a mixing bowl, mash the ripe bananas with a fork until smooth.

3. Add Melted Butter: Stir the melted butter into the mashed bananas.

4. Add Baking Soda and Salt: Sprinkle the baking soda and salt over the banana mixture, and stir until well combined.

5. Mix in Sugar, Egg, and Vanilla: Add the granulated sugar, beaten egg, and vanilla extract. Stir until everything is thoroughly combined.

6. Add Flour: Gradually add the all-purpose flour, stirring until just incorporated. Be careful not to overmix.

7. Fold in Chopped Nuts: Gently fold the chopped nuts into the batter. The nuts will add a delicious crunch to the bread.

8. Pour into Pan: Pour the batter into the greased loaf pan, spreading it evenly.

9. Bake the Bread: Bake in the preheated oven for about 60-65 minutes or until a toothpick inserted into the center comes out clean.

10. Cool and Serve: Let the banana nut bread cool in the pan for a few minutes, then transfer it to a wire rack to cool completely. Once cooled, slice and enjoy your delicious Banana Nut Bread!

Blueberry Muffins

Get ready to bake a berry-licious treat, junior bakers! Today, we're making Blueberry Muffins—a delightful, fruity breakfast or snack option.

Let's dive into this delicious baking adventure step by step:

Ingredients:
- 1 1/2 cups all-purpose flour
- 1/2 cup granulated sugar

- 2 teaspoons baking powder

- 1/2 teaspoon salt

- 1/2 cup milk

- 1/4 cup vegetable oil

- 1 large egg

- 1 cup fresh blueberries

Instructions:

1. Preheat the Oven: With help from a grown-up, preheat the oven to 400°F (200°C). Line a muffin tin with paper liners.

2. Mix Dry Ingredients: In a mixing bowl, whisk together the all-purpose flour, granulated sugar, baking powder, and salt.

3. Mix Wet Ingredients: In a separate bowl, whisk together the milk, vegetable oil, and egg until well combined.

4. Combine Wet and Dry Ingredients: Pour the wet mixture into the bowl of dry ingredients. Stir gently until just combined. It's okay if there are a few lumps.

5. Add Blueberries: Gently fold in the fresh blueberries. Be careful not to overmix, as it might break the blueberries.

6. Fill Muffin Cups: Using a spoon or ice cream scoop, divide the batter evenly among the muffin cups, filling them about two-thirds full.

7. Bake the Muffins: Bake in the preheated oven for about 18-20 minutes, or until a toothpick inserted into the center of a muffin comes out clean.

8. Cool and Enjoy: Let the blueberry muffins cool in the tin for a few minutes, then transfer them to a wire rack to cool completely. Once cooled, enjoy your homemade Blueberry Muffins!

Zucchini Chocolate Chip Bread

Get ready to bake a deliciously unique treat, junior bakers! Today, we're making Zucchini Chocolate Chip Bread—a moist and flavorful bread perfect for a sweet snack.

Let's dive into this delightful baking adventure step by step:

Ingredients:
- 1 1/2 cups all-purpose flour
- 1/2 teaspoon baking soda
- 1/2 teaspoon baking powder
- 1/2 teaspoon salt
- 1 teaspoon ground cinnamon
- 1/4 teaspoon ground nutmeg

- 1/2 cup granulated sugar

- 1/2 cup packed brown sugar

- 1/2 cup vegetable oil

- 2 large eggs

- 1 teaspoon vanilla extract

- 1 1/2 cups shredded zucchini (about one medium zucchini)

- 3/4 cup chocolate chips

Instructions:

1. Preheat the Oven: With help from a grown-up, preheat the oven to 350°F (175°C). Grease a 9x5-inch loaf pan.

2. Mix the Dry Ingredients: In a bowl, whisk together the all-purpose flour, baking soda, baking powder, salt, ground cinnamon, and ground nutmeg.

3. Mix the Wet Ingredients: In a separate bowl, whisk together the granulated sugar, brown sugar, vegetable oil, eggs, and vanilla extract until well combined.

4. Combine Wet and Dry Ingredients: Pour the wet mixture into the bowl of dry ingredients. Stir gently until just combined. It's okay if there are a few lumps.

5. Fold in Zucchini and Chocolate Chips: Gently fold the shredded zucchini and chocolate chips. The zucchini will add moisture, and the chocolate chips will add a sweet touch.

6. Pour into Pan: Pour the batter into the greased loaf pan, spreading it evenly.

7. Bake the Bread: Bake in the preheated oven for about 50-60 minutes or until a toothpick inserted into the center comes out clean.

8. Cool and Slice: Let the zucchini chocolate chip bread cool in the pan for a few minutes, then transfer it to a wire rack to cool completely.
Once cooled, slice and enjoy your homemade Zucchini Chocolate Chip Bread!

Cinnamon Swirl Muffins

Get ready to bake a swirl of deliciousness, junior bakers! Today, we're making Cinnamon Swirl Muffins—a perfect combination of tender muffins and sweet cinnamon goodness.

Let's dive into this delightful baking adventure step by step:

Ingredients for the Muffins:

- 2 cups all-purpose flour

- 1/2 cup granulated sugar

- 2 teaspoons baking powder

- 1/2 teaspoon baking soda

- 1/2 teaspoon salt

- 1 cup milk

- 1/4 cup vegetable oil

- 1 large egg

Ingredients for the Cinnamon Swirl:

- 1/4 cup granulated sugar

- 1 teaspoon ground cinnamon

Ingredients for the Streusel Topping:

- 1/4 cup all-purpose flour

- 1/4 cup granulated sugar

- 2 tablespoons cold butter, cubed

- 1/2 teaspoon ground cinnamon

Instructions:

For the Muffins:

1. Preheat the Oven: With help from a grown-up, preheat the oven to 375°F (190°C). Line a muffin tin with paper liners.

2. Mix the Dry Ingredients: In a mixing bowl, whisk together the all-purpose flour, granulated sugar, baking powder, baking soda, and salt.

3. Mix the Wet Ingredients: In a separate bowl, whisk the milk, vegetable oil, and egg until well combined.

4. Combine Wet and Dry Ingredients: Pour the wet mixture into the bowl of dry ingredients. Stir gently until just combined. It's okay if there are a few lumps.

5. Fill Muffin Cups: Using a spoon or ice cream scoop, fill each muffin cup with a small amount of batter, about one tablespoon.

For the Cinnamon Swirl:

1. Mix Cinnamon Swirl: Mix the granulated sugar and ground cinnamon for the swirl in a small bowl.

2. Add Swirl: Sprinkle a small amount of the cinnamon sugar mixture over the batter in each muffin cup.

For the Streusel Topping:

1. **Combine Streusel Ingredients:** In a bowl, combine the all-purpose flour, granulated sugar, cold butter cubes, and ground cinnamon. Use your fingers to mix the ingredients until you have a crumbly texture.

2. **Top with Streusel:** Sprinkle the Streusel mixture generously over the cinnamon-sugar layer in each muffin cup.

3. **Complete Muffin Batter:** Divide the remaining muffin batter evenly among the cups, covering the cinnamon-sugar layer and streusel topping.

Bake the Muffins:

1. Bake in the Oven: Bake in the preheated oven for about 15-18 minutes, or until a toothpick inserted into the center of a muffin comes out clean.

2. Cool and Enjoy: Let the cinnamon swirl muffins cool in the tin for a few minutes, then transfer them to a wire rack to cool completely. Once cooled, enjoy your homemade Cinnamon Swirl Muffins!

Pumpkin Spice Muffins

Get ready to bake a taste of autumn, junior bakers! Today, we're making Pumpkin Spice

Muffins—a delightful treat that captures the flavors of the season.

Let's dive into this cozy baking adventure step by step:

Ingredients for the Muffins:
- 1 3/4 cups all-purpose flour
- 1 teaspoon baking soda
- 1/2 teaspoon baking powder

- 1/2 teaspoon salt

- 1 teaspoon ground cinnamon

- 1/2 teaspoon ground nutmeg

- 1/2 teaspoon ground cloves

- 1/2 teaspoon ground ginger

- 1/4 cup unsalted butter, melted

- 1/2 cup granulated sugar

- 1/2 cup packed brown sugar

- 2 large eggs

- 1 cup canned pumpkin puree (not pumpkin pie filling)

- 1/4 cup milk

Ingredients for the Streusel Topping:

- 1/4 cup all-purpose flour

- 1/4 cup packed brown sugar

- 2 tablespoons unsalted butter, softened

- 1/2 teaspoon ground cinnamon

Instructions:

For the Muffins:

1. Preheat the Oven: With help from a grown-up, preheat the oven to 375°F (190°C). Line a muffin tin with paper liners.

2. Mix the Dry Ingredients: In a mixing bowl, whisk together the all-purpose flour, baking soda, baking powder, salt, ground cinnamon, ground nutmeg, ground cloves, and ground ginger.

3. Mix the Wet Ingredients: In a separate bowl, whisk together the melted butter, granulated sugar, brown sugar, eggs, pumpkin puree, and milk until well combined.

4. Combine Wet and Dry Ingredients: Pour the wet mixture into the bowl of dry ingredients. Stir gently until just combined. It's okay if there are a few lumps.

5. Fill Muffin Cups: Using a spoon or ice cream scoop, divide the batter evenly among the muffin cups, filling them about two-thirds full.

For the Streusel Topping:

1. Combine Streusel Ingredients: In a bowl, combine the all-purpose flour, packed brown sugar, softened butter, and ground cinnamon. Use your fingers to mix the ingredients until you have a crumbly texture.

2. Top with Streusel: Sprinkle the streusel mixture generously over the muffin batter in each cup.

Bake the Muffins:

1. Bake in the Oven: Bake in the preheated oven for about 18-20 minutes, or until a toothpick inserted into the center of a muffin comes out clean.

2. Cool and Enjoy: Let the pumpkin spice muffins cool in the muffin tin for a few minutes, then transfer them to a wire rack to cool completely. Once cooled, enjoy your homemade Pumpkin Spice Muffins!

Chapter 5: Fun and Fancy Treats

Homemade Pop Tarts

Get ready to bake a fun and tasty treat, junior bakers! Today, we're making Homemade Pop Tarts—a delightful pastry you can customize with your favorite fillings.

Let's dive into this exciting baking adventure step by step:

Ingredients for the Pastry Dough:

- 2 cups all-purpose flour

- 1 tablespoon granulated sugar

- 1/2 teaspoon salt

- 1 cup unsalted butter, cold and cubed

- 1/4 cup ice water

Ingredients for the Filling:

- Your choice of jam, preserves, Nutella, or other fillings

Ingredients for the Glaze:

- 1 cup powdered sugar

- 2 tablespoons milk

- Food coloring (optional)

Instructions:

For the Pastry Dough:

1. Mix the Dry Ingredients: In a mixing bowl, whisk together the all-purpose flour, granulated sugar, and salt.

2. Cut in the Butter: Add the cold, cubed butter to the flour mixture. Use a pastry cutter or your fingers to work the butter into the flour until you have a coarse, crumbly texture.

3. Add Ice Water: Gradually add the ice water, a tablespoon at a time, and mix until the dough starts to come together.

4. Form the Dough: Turn the dough onto a floured surface and knead it gently until it forms a cohesive ball. Divide the dough into two equal portions.

5. Roll Out the Dough: Roll out one portion of the dough into a rectangle about 1/8 inch thick.

6. Cut Out Rectangles: Cut the dough into rectangles of your desired size using a knife or a pastry cutter. These will be the bottom layers of your Pop-Tarts.

7. Assemble the Pop-Tarts: Place a small filling on each rectangle, leaving a border around the edges. Place another rectangle of dough on top of each filled rectangle.

8. Seal the Edges: Use a fork to press down and seal the edges of the rectangles, creating a crimped pattern.

9. Bake the Pop-Tarts: Place the assembled Pop-Tarts on a baking sheet lined with parchment paper. Bake in a preheated oven according to the size of your Pop-Tarts, typically around 15-20 minutes at 350°F (175°C) or until golden brown.

For the Glaze:

1. Mix the Glaze: Whisk together the powdered sugar and milk in a bowl until you have a smooth glaze. You can add food coloring to the glaze if you'd like to make it colorful.

2. Glaze the Pop-Tarts: Once the Pop-Tarts have cooled slightly, drizzle the glaze over the top. Allow the glaze to set before serving.

Mini Fruit Tarts

Get ready to create a burst of fruity goodness, junior bakers! Today, we're making Mini Fruit Tarts—a delightful and colorful treat that's as fun to make as it is to eat.

Let's dive into this delicious baking adventure step by step:

Ingredients for the Tart Shells:

- 1 1/4 cups all-purpose flour
- 1/4 cup granulated sugar
- 1/4 teaspoon salt
- 1/2 cup unsalted butter, cold and cubed
- 1 large egg yolk
- 1-2 tablespoons ice water

Ingredients for the Filling:

- Pastry cream or custard (store-bought or homemade)
- Assorted fresh fruits (berries, kiwi, mango, etc.)

Instructions:

For the Tart Shells:

1. Mix the Dry Ingredients: In a mixing bowl, whisk together the all-purpose flour, granulated sugar, and salt.

2. Cut in the Butter: Add the cold, cubed butter to the flour mixture. Use a pastry cutter or your fingers to work the butter into the flour until you have a coarse, crumbly texture.

3. Add Egg Yolk: Add the egg yolk and gently mix until the mixture starts to come together.

4. Add Ice Water: Gradually add the ice water, a tablespoon at a time, and mix until the dough forms a ball. Be careful not to overmix.

5. Form the Dough: Turn the dough onto a floured surface and gently knead it a few times to bring it together. Flatten the dough into a disc, wrap it in plastic wrap, and refrigerate for at least 30 minutes.

6. Roll Out the Dough: Roll out the chilled dough to about 1/8 inch thickness on a floured surface.

7. Cut Out Mini Tart Shells: Use a round cookie cutter to cut out circles from the rolled dough. Carefully press the circles into mini tart pans, pressing the dough into the edges and bottom.

8. Prick the Bottom: Prick the bottom of each tart shell with a fork to prevent it from puffing up during baking.

9. Bake the Tart Shells: Preheat the oven to 375°F (190°C). Place the tart shells on a baking sheet and bake for about 12-15 minutes or until golden brown. Let them cool completely.

Assemble the Mini Fruit Tarts:

1. Fill with Pastry Cream: Once the tart shells are cooled, fill each one with pastry cream or custard. You can use a spoon or a piping bag to fill them.

2. Arrange Fresh Fruits: Top the filled tart shells with assorted fresh fruits. Get creative with colorful combinations!

3. Serve and Enjoy: Your Mini Fruit Tarts are ready to be enjoyed. They are perfect for a light and refreshing dessert.

Chocolate-Dipped Pretzel Rods

Prepare to create a delightful combination of sweet and salty junior bakers! Today, we're making Chocolate-Dipped Pretzel Rods—a simple yet delicious treat for parties or snacking.

Let's dive into this fun and tasty baking adventure step by step:

Ingredients:

- Pretzel rods

- Chocolate chips (semi-sweet, milk, or white chocolate)

- Assorted toppings (sprinkles, crushed nuts, mini chocolate chips, etc.)

Instructions:

1. Melt the Chocolate: Melt the chocolate chips in a microwave-safe bowl or double boiler. If using the microwave, heat in 20-30 second intervals, stirring after each interval until the chocolate is smooth and fully melted.

2. Dip the Pretzel Rods: Hold a pretzel rod by one end and dip it into the melted chocolate, covering about two-thirds of the rod. Allow excess chocolate to drip off.

3. Add Toppings: While the chocolate is still wet, sprinkle your chosen toppings over the chocolate-dipped portion of the pretzel rod. Get creative and experiment with different toppings!

4. Place on Parchment Paper: Place the chocolate-dipped pretzel rods on a baking sheet lined with parchment paper. Make sure they are not touching each other.

5. Chill or Set: Depending on your preference and the temperature, let the chocolate set at room temperature or place the baking sheet in the refrigerator for a quicker setting.

6. Serve and Enjoy: Your Chocolate-Dipped Pretzel Rods are ready to be enjoyed once the chocolate is completely set. They make a wonderful treat for parties, celebrations, or simply as a sweet and salty snack.

Mini Cheesecakes with Fruit Topping

Get ready to create bite-sized creamy delights, junior bakers! Today, we're making Mini Cheesecakes with Fruit Topping—a delectable dessert combining rich cheesecake and colorful fruit toppings.

Let's dive into this delicious baking adventure step by step:

Ingredients for the Crust:

- 1 cup graham cracker crumbs

- 2 tablespoons granulated sugar

- 3 tablespoons unsalted butter, melted

Ingredients for the Cheesecake Filling:

- 2 (8-ounce) packages of cream cheese, softened

- 1/2 cup granulated sugar
- 1 teaspoon vanilla extract
- 2 large eggs

Ingredients for the Fruit Topping:

- Assorted fresh fruits (berries, kiwi, mango, etc.)
- Fruit jam or preserves for glaze (optional)

Instructions:

For the Crust:

1. Preheat the Oven: With help from a grown-up, preheat the oven to 325°F (160°C). Line a mini muffin tin with paper liners.

2. Mix Crust Ingredients: In a bowl, mix the graham cracker crumbs, granulated sugar, and melted butter until well combined.

3. Fill Crust: Place one teaspoon of the crumb mixture into the bottom of each mini muffin liner. Press down gently to form a crust layer.

For the Cheesecake Filling:

1. Mix Cheesecake Ingredients: In a mixing bowl, beat the softened cream cheese until smooth. Add the granulated sugar and vanilla extract, and mix until well combined.

2. Add Eggs: Add the eggs, one at a time, mixing well after each addition. The batter should be creamy and smooth.

3. Fill the Muffin Liners: Spoon the cheesecake batter into the muffin liners, filling them about three-quarters full.

4. Bake the Mini Cheesecakes: Bake the Mini Cheesecakes in the oven for 15-18 minutes or until the edges are set and the centers are slightly jiggly.

5. Cool and Chill: Allow the mini cheesecakes to cool in the muffin tin for a few minutes, then transfer them to the refrigerator to chill for at least 2 hours or until fully set.

For the Fruit Topping:

1. Prepare Fruits: Wash, peel, and chop your chosen fresh fruits for the topping.

2. **Optional Glaze:** Gently heat fruit jam or preserves and brush a thin layer over the chilled mini cheesecakes if desired. This adds a glossy finish and helps the fruits stick.

3. **Add Fresh Fruits:** Arrange the chopped fresh fruits on each mini cheesecake, creating colorful and eye-catching toppings.

Serve and Enjoy!

Cream Puffs with Vanilla Custard Filling

Get ready to create airy and creamy delights, junior bakers! Today, we're making Cream Puffs with Vanilla Custard Filling—a delectable pastry that will impress.

Let's dive into this delightful baking adventure step by step:

Ingredients for the Cream Puffs:

- 1/2 cup unsalted butter

- 1 cup water

- 1 cup all-purpose flour

- 4 large eggs

Ingredients for the Vanilla Custard Filling:

- 2 cups whole milk

- 1/2 cup granulated sugar

- 1/4 cup cornstarch

- 1/4 teaspoon salt

- 4 large egg yolks

- 1 teaspoon vanilla extract

Instructions:

For the Cream Puffs:

1. Preheat the Oven: With help from a grown-up, preheat the oven to 400°F (200°C). Line a baking sheet with parchment paper.

2. Prepare the Dough: Combine the butter and water in a saucepan. Bring to a boil. Add the flour all at once and stir vigorously until the mixture forms a ball and pulls away from the sides of the pan.

3. Cool the Dough: Remove the dough from the heat and let it cool for a few minutes.

4. Add Eggs: Add the eggs one at a time, beating well after each addition. The dough should become smooth and glossy.

5. Pipe the Dough: Transfer the dough to a piping bag fitted with a round tip. Pipe small mounds of dough onto the prepared baking sheet, leaving space between them.

6. Bake the Puffs: Bake in the preheated oven for about 20-25 minutes or until the cream puffs are puffed and golden brown. Let them cool completely on a wire rack.

For the Vanilla Custard Filling:

1. Prepare Vanilla Custard: Heat the whole milk over medium heat until it's steaming but not boiling.

2. Whisk Sugar, Cornstarch, and Salt: In a separate bowl, whisk together the granulated sugar, cornstarch, and salt. Add the egg yolks and whisk until smooth and slightly pale.

3. Temper the Egg Mixture: Gradually pour a small amount of the hot milk into the egg mixture while whisking constantly. This **"tempering"** prevents the eggs from curdling.

4. Combine and Cook: Pour the tempered egg mixture into the saucepan with the remaining milk. Cook over medium heat, whisking constantly, until the custard thickens and comes to a gentle boil.

5. Add Vanilla: Remove the custard from the heat and stir in the vanilla extract.

6. Cool and Chill: Let the custard cool slightly, then cover it with plastic wrap, pressing the wrap onto the surface to prevent skin from forming. Chill the custard in the refrigerator until it's completely cooled.

Fill the Cream Puffs:

1. Fill the Puffs: Once the cream puffs and the vanilla custard are cooled, use a piping bag fitted with a round tip to pipe the custard into the hollow centers of the cream puffs.

2. Serve and Enjoy: Your Cream Puffs with Vanilla Custard Filling are now ready to be enjoyed. They're a delightful combination of airy pastry and luscious custard!

Chapter 6: Creative Confections

Cake Pops: Bites of Joy

Cake Pop Creations to Try
- Classic Chocolate Delight
- Strawberry Shortcake Bliss
- Cookies and Cream Euphoria
- Tropical Pineapple Paradise

A. Classic Chocolate Delight

Ingredients for Classic Chocolate Delight Cake Pops:

- Chocolate cake (baked and cooled)
- Chocolate frosting
- Melting chocolate or candy coating (dark or milk chocolate)
- Optional: Chocolate sprinkles, cocoa powder for dusting

Instructions:

1. Prepare the Cake Base: Start by crumbling your cooled chocolate cake into fine crumbs using your fingers or a fork. In a mixing bowl, combine the cake crumbs with a generous amount of chocolate frosting.

The mixture should hold its shape when pressed together.

2. Shape the Cake Pops: Roll small portions of the cake mixture into bite-sized balls. Place the shaped balls on a parchment-lined tray and refrigerate them for about 20-30 minutes to firm up.

3. Melt the Chocolate: While the cake balls are chilling, melt your chocolate or candy coating according to the package instructions. Make sure it's smooth and ready for dipping.

4. Dip and Decorate: Dip the tip of a cake pop stick into the melted chocolate and then insert it into a chilled cake ball.

This will act as the anchor. Dip the cake ball into the melted chocolate, ensuring it's fully coated. Gently tap off any excess chocolate.

5. Set and Finish: Place the dipped cake pop upright in a styrofoam block or a cake pop stand. If desired, immediately sprinkle chocolate sprinkles over the wet chocolate coating. Let the chocolate set completely.

6. Optional Cocoa Dusting: For an extra touch of elegance, lightly dust the cake pops with cocoa powder once the chocolate coating is set.

7. Serve and Enjoy: Your "Classic Chocolate Delight" cake pops are now ready to be enjoyed! Arrange them on a decorative platter or package them individually for sharing.

B. Strawberry Shortcake Bliss

Ingredients for Strawberry Shortcake Bliss Cake Pops:

- Vanilla or strawberry cake (baked and cooled)
- Strawberry frosting
- Melting chocolate or candy coating (white or pink)
- Dried strawberry pieces or strawberry-flavored candy melts (for decorating)

Instructions:

1. Prepare the Cake Base: Crumble your cooled vanilla or strawberry cake into fine crumbs. In a mixing bowl, blend the cake crumbs with strawberry frosting until the mixture holds together when pressed.

2. Shape the Cake Pops: Roll small portions of the cake mixture into bite-sized balls. Place the shaped cake balls on a tray lined with parchment paper and refrigerate for about 20-30 minutes to firm up.

3. Melt the Chocolate: Melt the chocolate or candy coating according to the package instructions until it's smooth and ready for dipping.

4. Dip and Decorate: Dip the tip of a cake pop stick into the melted chocolate, then insert it into a chilled cake ball. This will serve as the anchor. Dip the cake ball into the melted chocolate, ensuring it's fully coated. Gently tap off any excess chocolate.

5. Decorate with Strawberry Flair: Before the chocolate coating sets, place a dried strawberry piece on top or drizzle strawberry-flavored candy melts over the cake pop for a burst of strawberry goodness.

6. Set and Enjoy: Carefully place the cake pop upright in a cake pop stand or styrofoam block and allow the chocolate to set completely.

7. Serve and Share: Your "Strawberry Shortcake Bliss" cake pops are now ready to be enjoyed! Arrange them on a plate or in a decorative container to showcase their delightful appearance and delectable flavor.

C. Cookies and Cream Euphoria

Ingredients for Cookies and Cream Euphoria Cake Pops:

- Chocolate or cookies and cream cake (baked and cooled)
- Cookies and cream frosting
- Melting chocolate or candy coating (white or dark chocolate)

- Crushed chocolate sandwich cookies (for mixing and decorating)

Instructions:

1. Prepare the Cake Base: Crumble your cooled chocolate, cookies, and cream cake into fine crumbs. In a mixing bowl, combine the cake crumbs with cookies and cream frosting until the mixture holds its shape when pressed together.

2. Mix in Crushed Cookies: Add a handful of crushed chocolate sandwich cookies to the cake mixture for an extra crunch and burst of cookie flavor. Mix them in until well combined.

3. Shape the Cake Pops: Roll small portions of the cake mixture into bite-sized balls. Place the shaped cake balls on a tray lined with parchment paper and refrigerate for about 20-30 minutes to firm up.

4. Melt the Chocolate: Melt the chocolate or candy coating according to the package instructions until it's smooth and ready for dipping.

5. Dip and Decorate: Dip the tip of a cake pop stick into the melted chocolate, then insert it into a chilled cake ball. This will anchor the cake pop. Dip the entire cake ball into the melted chocolate, ensuring it's fully coated. Gently tap off any excess chocolate.

6. Crushed Cookie Coating: While the chocolate coating is still wet, roll the cake pop in crushed chocolate sandwich cookies to create a textured and flavorful outer layer.

7. Set and Indulge: Carefully place the cake pop upright in a cake pop stand or styrofoam block and allow the chocolate to set completely.

8. Serve and Relish: Your "Cookies and Cream Euphoria" cake pops are now ready to be savored! Arrange them on a dessert platter or in decorative holders to showcase their delightful appearance and irresistible flavor.

D. Tropical Pineapple Paradise

Ingredients for Tropical Pineapple Paradise Cake Pops:

- Pineapple or coconut-flavored cake (baked and cooled)

- Pineapple Frosting

- Melting chocolate or candy coating (white or yellow)

- Dried pineapple pieces or toasted coconut flakes (for decorating)

Instructions:

1. Prepare the Cake Base: Crumble your cooled pineapple or coconut-flavored cake into fine crumbs.

In a mixing bowl, combine the cake crumbs with pineapple frosting until the mixture holds its shape when pressed together.

2. Shape the Cake Pops: Roll small portions of the cake mixture into bite-sized balls. Place the shaped cake balls on a tray lined with parchment paper and refrigerate for about 20-30 minutes to firm up.

3. Melt the Chocolate: Melt the chocolate or candy coating according to the package instructions until it's smooth and ready for dipping.

4. Dip and Decorate: Dip the tip of a cake pop stick into the melted chocolate, then insert it into a chilled cake ball.

This will anchor the cake pop. Dip the cake ball into the melted chocolate, ensuring it's fully coated. Gently tap off any excess chocolate.

5. Tropical Flair: Before the chocolate coating sets, place a piece of dried pineapple on top or sprinkle toasted coconut flakes over the cake pop to capture the essence of a tropical paradise.

6. Set and Enjoy: Carefully place the cake pop upright in a cake pop stand or styrofoam block and allow the chocolate to set completely.

7. Serve and Escape: Your "Tropical Pineapple Paradise" cake pops are ready to whisk you away on a culinary journey! Arrange them on a platter or in a decorative container, and let their vibrant appearance and delightful flavors transport you to a tropical retreat with every bite.

E. Cake Pop Creations to Try on Your Own

Get ready for a world of endless creativity and flavors, junior bakers! In this section, we're diving into the limitless possibilities of cake pop creations. From whimsical designs to unexpected flavor combinations, the possibilities are as vast as your imagination.

Inspiration for Your Cake Pop Creations:

1. Candyland Fantasy: Create cake pops that resemble colorful candies from a magical Candyland. Use bright candy melts, sprinkles, and edible glitter to make them pop with sweetness.

2. Fruity Fusion: Experiment with fruit-flavored cakes and coordinating frostings. Pair lemon cake with raspberry frosting or orange cake with passion fruit frosting for a burst of fruity delight.

3. Cookies Galore: Incorporate your favorite cookies into cake pop creations. Crushed Oreos, chocolate chip cookies, or even gingersnaps can add an exciting twist to your cake pops.

4. Charming Characters: Craft cake pops resembling beloved cartoon, movie, or storybook characters. Use edible decorations and fondant to bring these characters to life.

5. Seasonal Sensations: Embrace the seasons by creating cake pops that capture the essence of spring, summer, fall, or winter. Think blooming flowers, sunshiny faces, cozy leaves, and frosty designs.

6. Floral Elegance: Decorate your cake pops with edible flowers, petals, and floral designs. Think roses, daisies, and delicate blossoms that transform your treats into edible works of art.

7. Decadent Chocolate Combos: Elevate classic chocolate cake by pairing it with rich chocolate ganache or adding a surprise center of molten chocolate.

8. Mouthwatering Mocha: Infuse coffee flavor into your cake pops using mocha-flavored cake and coffee-infused frosting. Top with a sprinkle of cocoa or coffee grounds.

9. Nutty Delights: Incorporate crushed nuts like almonds, pistachios, or hazelnuts into your cake mixture for added crunch and flavor.

10. Rainbow Spectacle: Create vibrant cake pops using a rainbow of colors. Make each cake ball a different color, and dip them in coordinating colored coatings.

With each new creation, you can explore, experiment, and amaze with your cake pop skills. Happy baking and decorating, junior chefs! The adventure of cake pops is as boundless as your creativity!

Rice Krispie Treats with a Twist

Ingredients for Rice Krispie Treats with a Twist:

- Rice Krispie cereal
- Marshmallows
- Butter
- Flavored extracts or oils (such as vanilla, strawberry, or mint)
- Food coloring (optional)
- Additional mix-ins (chocolate chips, dried fruit, sprinkles, etc.)

Instructions:

1. Prepare the Base: Melt butter over low heat in a large saucepan. Add marshmallows and stir until fully melted and combined. Remove from heat.

2. Add Flavors and Colors: Stir in flavored extract or oil to infuse unique flavors into your treats. Add a few drops of food coloring and mix until evenly distributed for colorful twists.

3. Mix in Rice Krispie Cereal: Pour the Rice Krispie cereal into the marshmallow mixture and gently fold until all the cereal is coated.

This is the perfect time to add mix-ins like chocolate chips or dried fruit for added texture and flavor if desired.

4. Press into Pan: Transfer the mixture to a greased pan or baking dish. Use a spatula or your hands (greased with butter) to press the mixture evenly into the pan.

5. Cool and Cut: Allow the treats to cool and set before cutting them into squares or fun shapes using cookie cutters.

Flavorful Variations to Try:

1. Fruity Explosion: Add strawberry or raspberry extract to the marshmallow mixture and mix in dried fruit like cranberries or chopped dried strawberries for bursts of fruity goodness.

2. Minty Fresh: Infuse the treats with mint extract for a refreshing twist. Add mini chocolate chips for a flavor reminiscent of a mint chocolate chip dessert.

3. Cookies and Cream Crush: Mix in crushed chocolate sandwich cookies along with vanilla extract for a cookie and cream experience in every bite.

4. Caramel Delight: Stir caramel extract into the marshmallow mixture and mix in caramel bits for a rich and indulgent treat.

5. Rainbow Bliss: Divide the mixture into separate bowls, color each portion with a different hue, and layer them to create a vibrant rainbow effect.

These treats are perfect for parties, celebrations, or simply indulging in a delightful twist on a classic favorite.

Decorated Sugar Cookies

Ingredients for Decorated Sugar Cookies:

- Sugar cookie dough (store-bought or homemade)

- Royal icing (in various colors)

- Edible decorations (sprinkles, edible glitter, fondant shapes, etc.)

Instructions:

1. Prepare the Cookie Dough: Roll out your sugar cookie dough on a floured surface to your desired thickness.

Use cookie cutters to cut out shapes, and transfer them to a baking sheet lined with parchment paper.

2. Bake the Cookies: Follow the baking instructions for your sugar cookie dough to bake the cookies until they are golden around the edges. Let them cool completely before decorating.

3. Prepare Royal Icing: Mix up batches of royal icing in various colors using food coloring. Royal icing should be thick for outlining and thin for flooding. Use gel food coloring for vibrant colors.

4. Outline and Flood: Use a piping bag with a small round tip to outline the shape of your cookies with the thick royal icing. Let the outlines set for a few minutes.

Then, use a slightly thinned royal icing to "flood" or fill in the outlines, creating a smooth and even surface. Use a toothpick or small spatula to spread the icing.

5. Add Decorations: Add your chosen decorations while the flooded icing is still wet. This could be colorful sprinkles, edible glitter, or fondant shapes. You can also add details like swirls, dots, or patterns using different colors of royal icing.

6. Let Dry: Allow your decorated sugar cookies to dry completely. This can take several hours to overnight, depending on the humidity. Once the icing is fully set, your cookies can be enjoyed or packaged as gifts.

Decorative Ideas to Try:

1. Seasonal Splendor: Decorate cookies to match the seasons—snowflakes and mittens for winter, flowers and butterflies for spring, suns, and waves for summer, and leaves and pumpkins for fall.

2. Personalized Messages: Use letter-shaped cookie cutters to spell out names, messages, or fun phrases. Decorate the letters with colorful icing to create personalized treats.

3. Animal Friends: Create adorable animal-shaped cookies and bring them to life with royal icing details. Think cute faces, whiskers, and tiny eyes.

4. Fancy Florals: Craft beautiful floral designs using different shades of icing for petals and leaves. Add a touch of edible glitter to make your flowers sparkle.

5. Glamorous Geometrics: Experiment with geometric patterns like triangles, zigzags, and polka dots. Play with contrasting colors to make the designs pop.

Chocolate-Covered Marshmallow Pops

Ingredients for Chocolate-Covered Marshmallow Pops:

- Marshmallows (large size)
- Melting chocolate (milk, dark, or white)
- Decorative sprinkles, crushed nuts, or other toppings
- Lollipop sticks or sturdy paper straws

Instructions:

1. Prepare the Marshmallows: Carefully insert a lollipop stick or paper straw into each marshmallow. Ensure they're securely in place but don't push all the way through.

2. Melt the Chocolate: Melt your chocolate using a microwave or double boiler. Stir until it's smooth and free of lumps.

3. Dip and Decorate: Dip each marshmallow into the melted chocolate, ensuring it's fully coated. Let the excess chocolate drip off, and gently tap the stick on the side of the bowl to remove any additional drips.

4. Add Toppings: While the chocolate is still wet, sprinkle your chosen toppings over the coated marshmallow. This could be colorful sprinkles, crushed nuts, edible glitter, or mini chocolate chips.

5. Let Set: Place the chocolate-covered marshmallow pops on a parchment-lined tray or styrofoam block to allow the chocolate to set completely.

6. Serve and Enjoy: Once the chocolate is fully set, your Chocolate-Covered Marshmallow Pops are ready to be enjoyed! Arrange them in a decorative container or present them individually wrapped for a delightful treat.

Variation Ideas to Try:

1. S'mores Sensation: Roll the chocolate-coated marshmallows in crushed graham crackers for a s'mores-inspired delight.

2. Rainbow Magic: Dip the marshmallows in different colors of melted chocolate to create a rainbow effect. Add matching sprinkles for extra magic.

3. Chocolate Overload: Dip the marshmallows in chocolate, then drizzle with melted white or dark chocolate for a double chocolate extravaganza.

4. Fruity Fusion: Dip the marshmallows in flavored chocolate coatings, such as strawberry, orange, or mint, for a fruity freshness.

5. Elegant Drizzles: Dip the marshmallows in a rich chocolate coating and drizzle with contrasting colored chocolate for an elegant and artistic touch.

Fruit Kabobs with Yogurt Dip

Ingredients for Fruit Kabobs with Yogurt Dip:
- Assorted fresh fruits (strawberries, grapes, melon, pineapple, etc.)

- Wooden skewers or lollipop sticks

- Greek yogurt (plain or flavored)

- Honey or maple syrup (for sweetening)

- Optional: Chopped nuts, shredded coconut, or granola for topping

Instructions:

1. Prepare the Fruits: Wash and prepare the fresh fruits by cutting them into bite-sized pieces. Keep in mind that fruits like strawberries and pineapple should be easy to skewer.

2. Assemble the Kabobs: Thread the fruit pieces onto wooden skewers or lollipop sticks in any desired pattern. Get creative with color combinations and fruit shapes to make the kabobs visually appealing.

3. Prepare the Yogurt Dip: Mix Greek yogurt with a drizzle of honey or maple syrup in a small bowl to sweeten it to your taste. Stir until the sweetener is well incorporated.

4. Serve with Dip: Arrange the fruit kabobs on a serving platter and place the bowl of yogurt dip alongside.

You can also sprinkle chopped nuts, shredded coconut, or granola over the yogurt dip for added texture and flavor.

5. Enjoy and Share: Your Fruit Kabobs with Yogurt Dip are now ready to be enjoyed! Dip the fruit kabobs into the creamy yogurt dip and savor the flavors and textures.

Variation Ideas to Try:

1. **Tropical Paradise:** Create kabobs using tropical fruits like mango, kiwi, and papaya for a taste of the tropics.

2. **Berry Burst:** Combine various berries like strawberries, blueberries, and raspberries for a colorful and antioxidant-rich treat.

3. **Citrus Sunshine:** Use citrus fruits like orange segments and mandarin slices for a zesty and refreshing twist.

4. **Melon Medley:** Craft kabobs with various melons, such as watermelon, cantaloupe, and honeydew, for a juicy and hydrating treat.

5. Nutty Crunch: Roll the yogurt-covered kabobs in chopped nuts or granola for added crunch and flavor.

→ Next Page Mini Chocolate Fondue Party

Chapter 7: Special Occasion Sensations

Mini Chocolate Fondue Party

Ingredients for Mini Chocolate Fondue Party:

- Assorted dippables (strawberries, banana slices, marshmallows, pretzel sticks, etc.)

- Melting chocolate (milk, dark, or white)

- Optional: Crushed nuts, sprinkles, crushed cookies for toppings

Instructions:

1. Prepare the Dippables: Wash and prepare your assortment of dippable by cutting fruits into bite-sized pieces and arranging them on a platter. Make sure the dippables are dry to prevent the chocolate from seizing.

2. Melt the Chocolate: Melt the chosen chocolate using a microwave or double boiler. Stir until it's smooth and glossy.

3. Set Up the Fondue Station: Place the melted chocolate in a heat-safe bowl or a mini fondue pot. Set up a designated dipping area with a platter of dippables and fondue forks or skewers for dipping.

4. Dip and Decorate: Invite your friends to pick their favorite dippables and dip them into the melted chocolate. As the chocolate-coated treats are lifted, let them drip briefly before placing them on individual plates or parchment paper.

5. Add Toppings: While the chocolate is still wet, sprinkle crushed nuts, sprinkles, or crushed cookies over the coated dippables for added texture and flavor.

6. Enjoy the Fun: Dip, savor, and repeat! Please encourage your friends to experiment with different dippables and chocolate combinations to create their personalized treats.

Variation Ideas to Try:

1. **S'mores Extravaganza:** Offer graham crackers, marshmallows, and chocolate squares for a mini s'mores fondue party.

2. **Cookie Lover's Dream:** Provide an assortment of cookies (Oreos, biscotti, shortbread) for dipping, along with crushed cookies for extra texture.

3. **Nutty Indulgence:** Offer chopped nuts like almonds, pecans, and hazelnuts for a nutty twist on classic dippables.

4. **Crispy Crunch:** Include crispy treats like rice cereal squares, pretzel sticks, and potato chips for a salty-sweet combination.

5. Fruity Delight: Embrace a variety of fresh fruits for dipping, from berries to tropical delights like mango and kiwi.

Halloween Monster Cupcakes

Ingredients for Cupcakes:

- Cupcake batter (your choice of flavor)

- Buttercream frosting (colored in various Halloween hues)

- Candy eyeballs

- Colored gel icing (for details)

- Decorative sprinkles (optional)

Instructions:

1. Bake the Cupcakes: Prepare and bake your favorite cupcake batter according to the recipe. Let the cupcakes cool completely before decorating.

2. Color the Frosting: Divide your buttercream frosting into separate bowls and color them using Halloween-inspired colors like orange, green, purple, and black.

3. Frost the Cupcakes: Use a piping bag with a large round tip to frost the cupcakes with your colored buttercream frosting. Get creative with swirls, waves, and peaks.

4. Create Monster Faces: Use candy eyeballs to create the eyes of your monster cupcakes. Place them on the cupcakes in various positions to give each monster a unique look.

5. Add Details: Use colored gel icing to draw mouths, eyebrows, and other facial features on the cupcakes. Get imaginative with fangs, stitches, or zigzag smiles.

6. Sprinkle Magic: If desired, add decorative sprinkles like stars, bats, or even mini chocolate chips to enhance the Halloween theme.

Variation Ideas to Try:

1. Frankenstein's Creations: Craft cupcakes that resemble the famous monster using green frosting, candy eyes, and black gel icing for the iconic scar.

2. Mummy Mayhem: Wrap the cupcakes with white buttercream "bandages," leaving the candy eyes peeking out for a mummy-themed treat.

3. Vampire Vibes: Design cupcakes with red "blood" splatters using red gel icing and add vampire fangs for a spooky twist.

4. Spooky Spiders: Use black frosting to pipe spider legs onto the cupcakes and place candy eyeballs in the center for spider cupcakes.

5. Witchy Wonders: Decorate cupcakes with witch hat toppers made from colored fondant or chocolate and add green "warts" using green gel icing.

Snowman Cake for Winter Celebrations

Ingredients for Snowman Cake:

- Cake layers (your choice of flavor and shape)
- Buttercream frosting (white and various colors)
- Fondant (for details)
- Edible decorations (candy buttons, licorice, etc.)
- Powdered sugar (for a snowy effect)

Instructions:

1. Bake the Cake: Prepare and bake your cake layers according to the recipe. Allow them to cool completely before assembling and decorating.

2. Build the Snowman: Stack the cake layers, using buttercream frosting to hold them together. Use white buttercream to frost the entire cake for a snowy base.

3. Frosting Details: Use colored buttercream to create the snowman's hat, scarf, and buttons. Get creative with different colors for a festive touch.

4. Fondant Fun: Use fondant to shape the snowman's nose, eyes, mouth, and arms. Roll the fondant into various shapes and attach them to the cake using a dab of frosting.

5. Edible Accessories: Decorate the snowman cake with edible accessories like candy buttons for the eyes, a licorice scarf, or even chocolate candy for the hat.

6. Powdered Snow: Dust powdered sugar over the cake to create a snowy effect. This adds an extra touch of winter magic.

Variation Ideas to Try:

1. Snowy Landscape: Surround the snowman cake with a winter wonderland landscape made from coconut flakes, fondant trees, and powdered sugar "snow."

2. Frosty Friends: Craft a scene with multiple snowman figures, each with its personality and accessories.

3. Winter Forest: Create a forest of edible trees around the snowman cake using ice cream cones dipped in green-tinted buttercream and coated with green sprinkles.

4. Sledding Adventure: Position a fondant snowman on a fondant sled for an adorable scene of winter fun.

5. Snowflake Splendor: Decorate the cake with delicate fondant snowflakes for elegance and winter beauty.

Easter Bunny Cake

Ingredients for Easter Bunny Cake:

- Cake layers (your choice of flavor)

- Buttercream frosting (white and various colors)

- Fondant (for details)

- Edible decorations (candy eyes, chocolate eggs, etc.)

- Coconut flakes (for "fur")

Instructions:

1. Bake the Cake: Prepare and bake your cake layers according to the recipe. Allow them to cool completely before assembling and decorating.

2. Shape the Bunny: Stack and assemble the cake layers to form the bunny's body. Use white buttercream frosting to cover the entire cake as a base.

3. Ears and Face: Shape fondant into bunny ears and a bunny face. Attach them to the cake using a dab of frosting. Add fondant details for the bunny's nose, mouth, and whiskers.

4. Coconut Fur: Press coconut flakes onto the bunny's body to create a furry texture. Gently pat them onto the frosting to resemble bunny fur.

5. Decorate: Use colored buttercream to create the bunny's eyes, cheeks, and any additional details. Place candy eyes on the bunny's face for a cute touch.

6. Easter Basket: Decorate the bunny's paws with fondant or candy eggs to create the appearance of holding an Easter basket.

Variation Ideas to Try:

1. Floral Fantasy: Add fondant flowers or edible blooms around the bunny's ears or as accessories to celebrate the arrival of spring.

2. Carrot Delight: Position a fondant carrot near the bunny to create a playful, Easter-themed scene.

3. Egg-citing Adventure: Decorate the cake with colorful buttercream Easter eggs for a festive touch.

4. Bunny Friends: Create a group of bunny cakes in various sizes, each with its personality and expression.

5. Easter Bonnet: Design a fondant bonnet or hat for the bunny, complete with a ribbon or bow.

Fourth of July Firework Cookies

Ingredients for Fourth of July Firework Cookies:

- Sugar cookie dough (store-bought or homemade)

- Royal icing (in red, white, and blue)

- Edible glitter (optional)
- Small round piping tip (for icing)
- Toothpick (for creating firework bursts)

Instructions:

1. Prepare the Cookie Dough: Roll out your sugar cookie dough on a floured surface and cut out shapes using a star or circle cookie cutter. Transfer the shapes to a baking sheet lined with parchment paper.

2. Bake the Cookies: Follow the baking instructions for your sugar cookie dough and allow the cookies to cool completely.

3. Royal Icing Colors: Prepare batches of red, white, and blue royal icing using food coloring.

The consistency should be thick for outlining and thin for flooding.

4. Outline and Flood: Use a piping bag with a small round tip to outline the cookie shapes with the corresponding colored icing.

Allow the outlines to set for a few minutes, then use thinned icing to flood the inside of the outlines, creating a smooth surface.

5. Create Firework Bursts: While the flooded icing is still wet, use a toothpick to gently drag outward from the center of the icing, creating firework burst patterns.

You can create multiple bursts on each cookie using different colors.

6. Add Edible Glitter: While the icing is still wet, sprinkle edible glitter over the firework bursts for added sparkle and dimension.

Variation Ideas to Try:

1. Star-Spangled Night Sky: Create a backdrop of blue icing and add white star-shaped sprinkles to represent the night sky.

2. Colorful Explosion: Use multiple icing colors to create vibrant and multi-colored firework bursts on each cookie.

3. Patriotic Swirls: Experiment with swirled icing colors to create unique firework designs that resemble swirling bursts.

4. Bold and Bright: Use bold and contrasting colors like red, white, and electric blue to make the fireworks bursts pop.

5. Golden Glitter: Use gold edible glitter to add a touch of elegance and shine to your firework cookies.

Cake Parfait Delights

Ingredients for Cake Parfait Delights:

- Cake layers (your choice of flavor)

- Whipped cream or custard filling

- Fresh fruits, berries, or jam

- Optional: Crushed cookies, chocolate chips, caramel sauce

Instructions:

1. Prepare the Cake: Bake your favorite cake layers according to the recipe. Allow them to cool completely before assembling the parfaits.

2. Cut the Cake: Use a round cutter to cut circles or squares from the cake layers to fit your serving glasses or cups.

3. Layer the Goodness: Begin by placing a cake layer at the bottom of each glass. Top it with a dollop of whipped cream or custard filling.

4. Add Fruit Bliss: Add a layer of fresh fruits, berries, or a spoonful of jam on top of the cream. This adds a burst of fruity goodness to your parfait.

5. Repeat the Layers: Continue layering with another piece of cake, more cream, and more fruits. Repeat the process until the glass is nearly filled, finishing with a final layer of cream.

6. Top with Delights: Finish off your cake parfait with a sprinkling of crushed cookies, chocolate chips, or a drizzle of caramel sauce.

Variation Ideas to Try:

1. Chocolate Lover's Parfait: Layer chocolate cake with chocolate mousse and top with chocolate shavings.

2. Berrylicious Delight: Alternate layers of vanilla cake with mixed berries and top with a dollop of whipped cream.

3. Tropical Escape: Layer coconut cake with diced pineapple and mango, and top with toasted coconut flakes.

4. Cookies and Cream Dream: Use chocolate cake layers with crushed cookies and layers of whipped cream for an indulgent treat.

5. Caramel Apple Parfait: Combine spiced apple cake with caramel sauce and chunks of cooked apples for a taste of autumn.

Conclusion

Your Baking Adventure Continues!

Congratulations, junior bakers, on completing your journey through **"The Junior Baker's Cookbook: Sweet Treats and Creative Confections."** From classic cookies and cupcakes to cake parfaits and beyond, you've explored a world of delightful flavors, creative designs, and sweet memories. But this is just the beginning of your baking adventure!

Remember, every recipe you've learned is a canvas waiting for your unique touch. Feel free to experiment with flavors, colors, and decorations to create your signature treats. Baking is all about having fun, embracing creativity, and sharing your delicious creations with loved ones.

As you continue baking, don't be afraid to try new recipes, explore different techniques, and let your imagination run wild. The joy of baking is not just in the final treat but in mixing, measuring, and creating something special from scratch.

Thank you for embarking on this delicious adventure with "The Junior Baker's Cookbook." Your passion for baking will grow stronger, and your kitchen will become a hub of inspiration and delight.

So, grab your apron, mixing bowls, and your sense of wonder, because your baking adventure continues to unfold!

Happy baking, junior chefs, and may your kitchen always be filled with the sweet aroma of creativity and joy.

With love and floury fingers,

[Sharon D. Morgan]

Experimenting With Your Own Flavors and Ideas

Junior bakers, you've gained a treasure trove of baking knowledge and recipes from "The Junior Baker's Cookbook." But guess what? The fun is just getting started! One of the most exciting parts of being a baker is the endless opportunity to experiment and create your flavors, designs, and treats.

As you step into your baking adventures, here are a few tips to help you unleash your inner baking genius:

1. Start with the Basics: Experiment with small tweaks to your favorite recipes. Try adding different extracts, spices, or even a touch of citrus zest to see how flavors evolve.

2. Mix and Match: Feel free to combine your favorite flavors. Chocolate and peanut butter? Vanilla and raspberry? The possibilities are endless!

3. Texture Play: Experiment with textures by adding nuts, dried fruits, or crunchy bits like cereal or crushed cookies to your treats.

4. Color Magic: Use natural food coloring or colorful fruits to add vibrant hues to your creations. Create a rainbow of cupcakes or cookies that are as beautiful as they are tasty.

5. Design Delights: Dream up your own decorations and designs. Create unique frosting swirls, intricate patterns, or even edible characters that make your treats stand out.

6. Inventive Fillings: Surprise everyone with unexpected fillings in your cupcakes or cakes. Think about jams, custards, or even gooey caramel centers.

7. Get Inspired: Look around you for inspiration. Nature, books, movies, and your favorite colors can spark new ideas for delightful treats.

8. Document Your Adventures: Keep a baking journal or digital notes of your experiments. Note what worked, what didn't, and how you'd like to adjust things next time.

9. Share and Savor: Remember to share your creations with friends and family. Their feedback can help you refine your recipes and make them even better.

Remember, there's no right or wrong in baking when you're experimenting with flavors and ideas.

Each experiment is a learning opportunity, and even if things don't turn out exactly as planned, you'll gain valuable insights that will make you a better baker.

So, young culinary explorers, sprinkle your imagination into your mixing bowls. Embrace the joy of creating, tasting, and sharing your unique treats.

Your baking journey is limitless, and your delicious discoveries are waiting. Happy experimenting, and may your creativity always be as boundless as your passion for baking!

Keep baking and keep shining, junior chefs!

Sharing Your Delicious Creations with Friends and Family

Junior bakers, one of the sweetest joys of your baking adventure is sharing the delicious treats you've lovingly crafted with friends and family.

The smiles, the "oohs" and "aahs," and the delighted expressions on their faces make your efforts all the more rewarding.

Here are some wonderful ways to spread the happiness of your baking creations:

1. Family Dessert Night: Turn an ordinary evening into a memorable event by surprising your family with a spread of your homemade treats. Set up a mini dessert buffet and let everyone indulge in your sweet delights.

2. Bake Sales: Organize a bake sale at school or in your community to raise funds for a good cause. People will love purchasing and savoring your treats while supporting a meaningful initiative.

3. Celebrations: Birthdays, holidays, and special occasions are the perfect times to showcase your baking talents. Craft treats that match the event's theme, and watch them become the star of the celebration.

4. Picnic Pleasures: Pack a basket of your baked goods and head outdoors for a picnic. Your friends and family will appreciate your effort in making the day even more special.

5. Gifts from the Heart: Surprise your loved ones with a box of homemade treats as a thoughtful and delicious gift. Wrap them with a ribbon and a handwritten note for an extra special touch.

6. Baking Parties: Host a baking party with friends and show them the ropes of creating delicious treats. Everyone can take home their own delicious masterpieces.

7. Sharing with Neighbors: Spread kindness in your neighborhood by sharing your baked goods with your neighbors. A plate of freshly baked cookies can brighten someone's day.

8. Virtual Treat Time: In this digital age, you can even share your baking successes online with friends and family who are far away. Post pictures, recipes, and baking tips on social media to inspire others.

Remember, when you share your baking creations, you're not just giving a taste of your treats—you're sharing a piece of your passion, creativity, and the joy that goes into each bite. Your baking can create wonderful memories and bring smiles to those around you.

So, keep measuring, mixing, and baking with love. Whether you're crafting cookies, cupcakes, or a cake masterpiece, know that each delightful bite is a way of spreading joy and connecting with others through the magic of baking.

Happy sharing and happy baking, junior chefs!